ROD MATTHEWS

CHANGE
THE MECHANICS OF PERSONAL TRANSFORMATION
STARTS HERE

First published by Impact Publishing 2011

A CIP catalogue of this book is available from the National Library of Australia.

ISBN 978-0-9775519-1-0

Project managed by Messenger Publishing
PO Box H241, Australia Square, NSW 1215
www.themessengergroup.com.au

Illustrations by Kristin Hardiman.

Printed in China.

CONTENTS

INTRODUCING THE AUTHOR

As an author, facilitator, presenter and the principal of Impact Human Performance Technologies, Rod Matthews has spent the past 15 years working nationally and internationally changing individuals, groups and organisations.

As there is only so much of Rod to go around, his regular clients include AUSTAR Entertainment, Avon, Deloitte, Hewitt Associates, Logica, Merck Serono, Roche and The University of New England.

Rod is a voracious reader of nerdy non-fiction and loves testing what he finds in books, articles and websites in the real world. This has a tendency to make it difficult for Rod to get invited to dinner parties and barbecues. So now Rod balances this with a good dose of comic fiction, swimming, playing football (soccer ... the real football), and spending time with his family and friends who allow him to attend barbecues mostly out of a sense of community service.

Frequently referred to as 'the best trainer in Australia', Rod's courses are thought provoking, insightful, interactive and hilarious.

Rod has also authored several other books including:

- *Practical Performance Improvement*, an incredibly practical approach to leading and improving the performance of team members.

- *Precision Recruitment Skills*, a step-by-step guide to seeing beyond a candidate's polished interview techniques to uncover the real person.

- *The Creative Edge – Strategies for 24/7 Creativity*. As a guest author, Rod covers the 'how to', 'want to' and 'chance to' of creativity.

For more information, visit www.rodmatthews.com

ACKNOWLEDGEMENTS

Most of what we know is a result of the amalgamation of personal experience, conversations with others and reading over many years. We all stand on the shoulders of others. With this in mind, it would be impossible to acknowledge every person who has truly contributed to this book.

Other authors, team members, course participants, colleagues, friends and family have all played a role in building the book.

There are, however, some people in particular that I must mention.

Firstly to Dr Martin E. P. Seligman whose depth and breadth of work is truly astonishing. He has published a small library of books including the highly influential *Learned Optimism* which I draw on heavily in Chapter 2. He is also the founder of Positive Psychology and is the patron of many projects in schools, universities and communities that are improving the life of millions of people. He is a bloody champion and will be quoted among the greats for many years to come.

Viktor Frankl, who sadly passed away in 1997, remains one of the most inspirational figures in modern times. As a neurologist and psychologist, his work paved the way for many who followed. Combine an academic rigour with his experience as a holocaust survivor and the result is some of the most poignant work available in the field of human studies.

Thanks and recognition must also go to Reinhold Niebuhr, the American theologian, author and commentator on public affairs whose 'serenity prayer' has become a universal proverb.

The works of many people have been an inspiration. In particular, for this book, I would furthermore like to acknowledge the following people: Mahatma Gandhi, the political and ideological leader of India and its bid for freedom; Virginia Satir, the American author and family therapist for her insight and eye for detail; Jim Loehr and Tony Swartz, whose work in human performance remains a benchmark; Scott Volkers, the head of Queensland Swimming and coach of a number of Olympians; Paul D. MacLean, the eminent physician and neuroscientist; Malcolm Gladwell, the author whose knack of being able to make research readable is helping educate millions; Dr Richard Davidson at the University of Wisconsin, Dr Paul Ekman of the University of California and Dr Dan Siegel of Havard University for their work into meditation, the brain and behaviour ... may their research continue to reveal its insights.

I would also like to thank Kristin Hardiman who has developed an entire art gallery for Impact Human Performance Technologies. The sheer breadth of her artistic portfolio is among the most impressive I have seen. We reproduce a small amount of her work in this book with her kind permission.

To my family, Margaret, Liam and Riley, thank you for all your love, support and honesty. And thank you for putting all things into perspective.

Many thanks to Tim Bedding, Tony Hall, Robert Scanlon and Peta Bayman. If I had to choose people to be trapped with on a deserted island, you would be on the list because of your insight, wit and conversation.

Thanks also to my Mum and Dad ... the most devoted, patient and supporting teachers I'll ever know. I miss you Mum.

HOW TO GET THE MOST OUT OF THIS BOOK

Impact Human Performance Technologies has designed this and all its books with this saying in mind:

> I hear and I forget,
> I see and I remember,
> I do and I understand!

Our books are best read with a pencil in hand so that you are ready to take part in practical activities and exercises, and to record your thoughts, feelings and experiences. To get the most out of this book, please be prepared to participate, record and reflect as well as read.

The aim of this book is to provide you with lots of tips, tools and techniques that actually work! There are a variety of ways you can use it:

• Self-paced learning

This book is put together in a way that will allow you and/or your work colleagues to complete the learning at your own pace.

• Training tool

Please feel free to copy the material in this book to form part of your training sessions or workshops. All we ask is that you reference the material with '© 2011, Rod Matthews, Impact Human Performance Technologies'.

• Learning resource

All of the Impact books combined form an excellent library for any business interested in investing in its workforce or for any individual interested in investing in his or her own education.

INTRODUCTION

At the beginning of a book such as this I can understand that you might be thinking a number of different things. For example, you might be thinking …

> *The last thing this world needs is another self-help book. Book stores are full of books that are full of meaningless drivel of zero use* – Vibrating at Level Indigo, How to Win Every Time and Not be a Social Exile, *or* Self Actualisation through Macramé.

Or you might be thinking …

> *Great, a book on how to change for the better! I know exactly who to give this to and I sincerely hope they read it and change. After all, it's the rest of the world that is mad …*

Or you might be thinking …

> *Listen Rod, I've been around. I've changed many times without any help. So I know how to change. What could you possibly talk about that I don't already know?*

No matter what you are thinking or feeling at this point, a couple of things are for sure. The information in this book will provide you with an excellent opportunity to do a few things:

Firstly, to understand and practise the criteria that wise people use to know when they are able to take control of a situation or when they would be best served by going with the flow.

Secondly, to look at what it is you can do to reduce the number of times you find yourself walking away from a situation thinking, 'If only I'd said ...' or 'If only I'd done ...' and to increase the number of times you respond to a difficult situation or an opportunity in a way that you are proud of.

And thirdly, you have an opportunity to increase your level of calm, comfort and centredness with those situations in life that you cannot control.

At work

In some respects it is easy to change an organisation's public profile, its strategy, and its policies, procedures and systems. The real challenge begins when we ask people to support the public profile, to understand the strategy, to apply the policy, to follow the procedure or to use the system.

Changing people fascinates me. For more than 15 years I have been fortunate enough to work with organisations to change individual, group and organisational behaviours. Some clients want to stop doing things that are derailing their own or others' careers, others want to adopt the behaviours that will allow them to achieve their goals or prepare them as leaders ready for new heights.

Working with people to improve their performance, I have found myself having many conversations with many people in many different circumstances – conversations about how to change, improve, build, motivate, communicate, persuade and generally get things done for themselves or with others.

These conversations start easily enough. People are, obviously, often quite engaged in their own stuff and are happy to talk about what is and isn't working well. At some point during many conversations we hit a familiar wall – for the universal truth is that there are some things that cannot be changed. I often found myself arriving at the point where the only thing left to say was, 'Well … grant me the courage to change what I can, the serenity to live with what I cannot and the wisdom to know the difference.'

When you say this in such a conversation it is a bit like a full stop. The conversation comes to a halt as all parties nod sagely, but the implied suggestion is usually that nothing can be done and that's that!

After a while I started to wonder what the criteria would be for what we can and cannot change and how exactly to be courageous and serene. Wouldn't it be great if, when things happen, we could evaluate the event against a list of principles and know whether we can or cannot have an effect on the outcome? We would then know if we needed to be courageous or serene and exactly how to do that!

One of the wonderful things about your brain is that if you ask it a question, often enough it starts to find answers.

With family

When my wife Margaret was pregnant with our first child I can remember reading an article in a newspaper that had a list of suggested things you should do before you have children. The list included things like:

- buy and read the Sunday paper in peace and quiet
- enjoy a leisurely bath
- take your partner to dinner at a posh restaurant.

The suggestion that stuck most in my mind was the one that said to gather all your friends and family who already have children and tell them where they are going wrong as parents … because it is the last time you will have all the answers.

I knew that parenting would be challenging and the rules would be constantly changing. It soon became obvious as a parent that just knowing what you can and cannot change is not enough. You need to do something with that knowledge. You need to be able to be courageous or serene.

Every moment, every day

As people age, their bodies take them on a journey from being 10 feet tall and bulletproof through to being old and frail. When you are young you fall over, when you are old you 'have a fall'. Along the way it is difficult to not notice what is happening.

If Charles Darwin is right, there must be an evolutionary benefit to all this. As men grow older, they stop growing hair on their heads and start growing it from their nostrils and ears. Women just start growing facial hair! I complained about the brutality of ageing to my wife one morning. She listened patiently but when I'd finished she reminded me of our neighbour who had passed away from breast cancer the previous Christmas Eve, leaving behind a husband and three gorgeous kids. She finished by saying, 'Rod, growing old is a privilege.'

Every time you come face to face with mortality you gain an appreciation of the time you have. Life is too short to live unconsciously.

The aim of the book

After 10 years of research, experimentation, presentations, and meeting thousands of course participants with whom I discussed and tested ideas, I have developed and fine-tuned the material in this book.

I have been fortunate enough to witness the transformation of hundreds of people and still get a buzz when I catch up with someone who has used this information to change their attitudes, behaviours, results and their lives.

Viktor Frankl, a pioneering neurologist, psychiatrist and holocaust survivor, once famously said:

> Between stimulus and response there is a space. In that space is our power to choose our response. In our response lies our growth and our freedom …

This book identifies the criteria wise people use to determine whether they have any control over a situation. It also provides us with the tools to help expand that moment between stimulus and response and to create ways to be courageous and serene that can be replicated.

One.

TRIGGER HAPPY

Turning a bad day into a good day

'... for there is nothing either good or bad, but thinking makes it so.'

William Shakespeare, *Hamlet*, Act 2, Scene 2

Slowly, dream becomes reality. Consciousness edges out unconsciousness. Sleep recedes and you become aware of your surroundings. Cocooned in your bedclothes, your eyes momentarily blink open and a cloud of thought drifts across your mind. 'It seems lighter at this time of morning than it normally is.' The thought stays like an unwelcome guest after a party. This thought has more to say. You turn to examine the thought when you realise that your alarm has not gone off and it is a work day.

A battlefield of curses, problems and questions follows you from bed to shower, wardrobe to car like six-year-olds around a football. 'Why didn't the alarm go off? What have I got on today? What's the time now? The traffic is going to be horrendous. I'm meant to be at a meeting! Do I have time for a shower? Did I mix up AM and PM on the alarm? Which route will have the least traffic? Can I fake an illness and call in sick? I wonder if Dr Who would let me borrow his tardis.' The cursing escalates as you remember that today was an important day. You have a meeting with the boss and a potential new client and you are scheduled to make a presentation. Perhaps seeking political asylum in a foreign country that does not have extradition arrangements is the best option.

You manage to weave through traffic at the breakneck speed of 30km/h and you almost feel a sense of relief as you get a good two cars ahead of where you were. And then you come to a grinding halt where, if past experience is anything to go by, you will stay for quite some time. You now accept that you will indeed be late and unable to present at the all-important meeting.

You look for your phone to call your boss so you can at least give her enough time to find your presentation and make a go of it without you. But your phone is not on the seat, the console, in your bag or, it starts to dawn on you, anywhere in the car. You have left your phone at home. You picture it on your bedside table anxiously vibrating as if voicing your boss's growing frustration.

Angry and helpless, you try to remember all the self-help books you have ever read. But in this context it just seems easier to repeat cynical self-affirmations; deep breathing just leads to hyperventilating and, in this traffic, you could count to 10 over 900 times and still have enough adrenaline to wrestle an ape.

So ... how do you turn a day like this around? How do you 'do' a good day?

It sounds like a ridiculous question at first. You might be thinking that a good day is something that just happens, something that you are on the receiving end of, something that is dependent on many variables coming together and subject to things outside your control. In some respects you are right.

There are some things that happen in our lives that we have no control over, and yet their effect on our lives (let alone on one day of one life) is phenomenal. Where we are born, the family we grow up with, the loss of someone close to us … our degree of control over some of these things is, at best, nil.

What we can do, however, is look at the following factors:

- how we respond when these things happen
- what we can do to reduce the recurrence of triggers for a bad day
- what we can do to increase the number of triggers for a great day
- how we can change our thoughts, feelings and behaviours to get better results for ourselves and for those around us.

Let's put these things to one side for a moment – we shall revisit them later. We can begin to see how to 'do' a good day by first answering the question … how do we do a *bad* day?

Where does it all start?

Most people would agree that a bad day starts with some event, often external to our control. This could be called a *trigger*.

In the opening example there were a number of triggers stitched together:

- the alarm not going off
- being late for a meeting
- getting caught in traffic
- leaving the phone at home.

Other examples include:

- receiving bad news
- rain ruining your plans
- it taking twice as long as usual to get the kids out of the house to school
- having a hangover and remembering what you did last night … up to a certain point
- pouring milk into your morning cup of coffee only to have it come out in lumps.

In the space provided below, note down what you would be thinking to yourself and how you would be feeling if you had a morning where a number of these triggers all happened in a row (be sure to take the time to jot these down – we will come back to this and other exercises later in the book):

Chances are that most people would be thinking things along the lines of 'Today's going to be a bad day', 'I should have stayed in bed' or 'Today should be a doona day' and feeling stressed and tense.

Triggers ➔ *Attitudes*

So triggers (such as no alarm, no breakfast, a traffic jam and being late for a meeting) will lead to certain thoughts and feelings or, for the sake of this book, *attitudes* (such as 'Today's going to be a bad day', 'I should have stayed in bed' or 'I'm feeling stressed and tense').

The next step is to identify how you behave when these attitudes arise.

In the space provided below, note down how you would be walking the last couple of metres to work; how you might respond to people saying 'Good morning', or what you might do when you arrive at your work area if you were thinking 'Today's going to be a bad day' or 'I should have stayed in bed' and feeling stressed and tense:

Once again, chances are that most people would be walking in a 'Today's a bad day' way using the following body language:

- head down
- frowning
- perhaps walking faster than normal in an angry fashion
- perhaps walking slower than normal in a defeated fashion
- avoiding eye contact with others
- mumbling menacingly and occasionally breaking out into maniacal laughter.

When other people say 'Good morning' you might respond in these ways:

- with fewer words, for example 'Hello' rather than 'Hello, how are you today?'
- in a less melodic tone of voice than usual
- with less eye contact
- you might even be a little cynical or rude with your response: 'What's so good about this morning?'

Triggers ➜ *Attitudes* ➜ *Behaviours*

So … you arrive at the office and, because the meeting is over, you go directly to your desk. Your email inbox looks like a virus has taken control of your computer and the messages all seem to be marked urgent. You check your voice messages – there are three important calls and a terse message from your boss asking where you are.

As you start to deal with the emails a workmate walks in and says, 'We've got a problem. I need you to look at this straightaway.'

Once again the behaviours you choose to use at this stage could range from rudeness through to passive aggression:

- keeping your fingers on the computer keyboard while he talks
- giving him minimal eye contact while still typing away
- answering him with sentences of seven words or less: 'Yep. I don't mind. Whatever. If you think so. That's fine.'
- giving a forced smile
- saying 'Yep, yep, yep' over the top of his explanation
- sighing and rolling your eyes as he explains what is going on
- saying 'Well, this was nice but gosh is that the date?'

All these behaviours will make it very clear to the other person that you are not interested in what he is talking about. Only the most evolved of workmates is going to say something like, 'You seem a little distracted. Is everything okay?' These workmates only exist in badly scripted training videos. In real life they are certainly on the endangered species list.

The fact of the matter is that most workmates will just shake their heads as they walk out, roll their eyes at other team members and swap stories about how much of a jerk you are while they unite against the common enemy … YOU!

The net result is that people will approach you in a way that suggests you *are* having a bad day and you *are* in a bad mood.

Don't be surprised if they do the following:

- force a smile when dealing with you
- speak to you in sentences of seven words or less. 'Yep. I don't mind. Whatever. If you think so. That's fine.'
- precede what they want to tell you with phrases such as 'Look, you're not going to like this, but …', 'I know you're having a bad day today, but …', 'Now don't get cranky at me when I tell you this …'
- find reasons to not talk to you
- send you an email even though they are at the next desk
- wait until you are out of the office before dropping things on your desk
- pick up the phone and pretend to be talking to someone as you approach them.

As you walk away you think to yourself, 'See, today is a bad day. Even my workmates have got it in for me.'

Triggers ➔ *Attitudes* ➔ *Behaviours*
➔ *Results*

All these behaviours only serve to reinforce your current attitude, that 'Today's going to be a bad day.' As a result of our attitudes and behaviours, the quality of the day becomes a self-fulfilling prophecy.

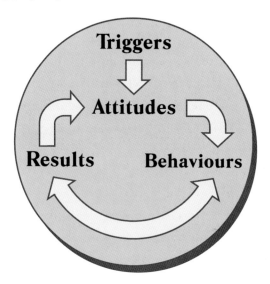

Triggers:

- alarm doesn't go off
- caught in traffic
- late for a meeting

Attitudes:

- 'Today's going to be a bad day'
- 'I should have stayed in bed'
- feeling stressed and tense

Behaviours:

- walking with head down and frowning
- perhaps walking faster than normal in an angry fashion
- perhaps walking slower than normal and looking defeated
- when talking to workmates: responding with fewer words, in a less melodic way than normal, and perhaps with less eye contact than usual.

Results:

- people force a smile when dealing with you
- people speak to you in sentences of seven words or less. 'Yep. I don't mind. Whatever. If you think so. That's fine.'
- people precede what they want to tell you with phrases like 'Look, you're not going to like this, but …', 'I know you're having a bad day today, but …', 'Now don't get cranky at me, but …'
- increased error rates and reworking due to the fact that people are avoiding you and finding reasons not to talk to you.

How do you do a *good* day?

The reverse of the above scenario therefore applies for being able to 'do' a good day.

Let's leave the triggers aside for a moment. We will revisit them later.

Imagine for a moment you are thinking to yourself that today is going to be a good day. You are feeling a little more buoyant than usual, on top of things and ready for pretty well anything.

In the space provided below, note down how you would be walking the last couple of metres to work, how you might respond to people saying 'Good morning', what you might do when you arrive at your work area, if you are thinking 'Today's going to be a great day!' and feeling enthused and ready:

Once again, chances are that most people would be walking in a 'Today's a great day!' way:

- head up
- smiling
- perhaps walking faster than normal in a purposeful fashion
- perhaps walking slower than normal in a relaxed and comfortable manner

- or maybe even singing, skipping and showering people in rose petals …

When other people say 'Good morning' you might respond:

- with more words, for example 'Hello Daniel. How are you today?' rather than just 'Hello'
- in a more melodic tone of voice
- with confident and comfortable eye contact.

When you arrive at the office and start to deal with your emails, a workmate walks in and says, 'We've got a problem. I need you to look at this straightaway.'

If you were thinking 'Today's going to be a great day' and feeling enthused and ready, you are more likely to respond like this:

- turn to give him your full attention
- smile as you ask him what it is you need to look at
- involve him in a conversation that works to solve the issue together.

These behaviours will generate a very different result. For example:

- the workmate smiles and thanks you as he walks out
- he talks about how great you are to work with at the coffee machine or water cooler
- less errors and reworking result as people are happy to keep you in the loop
- you will be thinking, 'Today is going to be a good day. I have already headed off a possible crisis.'

So, attitudes lead to behaviours that lead to results that lead to attitudes that lead to behaviours that lead to results that lead to attitudes and so on. It is a self-perpetuating cycle that can be either a downward or an upward spiral.

When bad things happen

Now, I can understand that the more cynical among you might be thinking, at this stage, something like:

> Ah yes, the power of positive thinking! Very good, Rod, but sadly impractical. Bad things do happen. Let's just change the context a little and see how your theory holds up. Let's say that you have just bought a new car. You are driving it out of the showroom when you stop at the first set of traffic lights and the person behind you doesn't see you and runs up the back of the car. Are you seriously suggesting that I should get out of the car, shake the other driver by the hand and say, 'Thank you. Thank you so much. What an excellent opportunity to get the car resprayed!'

Well, you could try that ... but you might find yourself hugging yourself in a white jacket with belts and very long sleeves.

Bad things do happen. More than that, horrific things happen and on many of these occasions it is difficult to see any link between human and humane. When bad things happen, nothing we say or do after the fact is going to change the reality that bad things have happened.

I'm not suggesting that when bad things happen you should respond inappropriately. What I am suggesting is that how we respond when bad things happen will make all the difference to us and those around us.

To illustrate this a little further, allow me to introduce you to my two sons Liam and Riley. The boys are about two years apart in age, with the combined energy of 14 adults and the curiosity of a roomful of cheeky monkeys.

One afternoon when Liam was six and Riley was four, Liam was watching TV in the lounge room while Riley was fossicking around in the kitchen. All of a sudden there was an enormous crash in the kitchen. When I walked in, Riley was standing on a chair surrounded by broken glass and lollies. The lolly jar we kept in the pantry was smashed on the ground and Riley had been caught red-handed.

'What happened, Riley?' I asked.

Riley's first response was to *deny* that there was a problem:

'What? What do you mean?'

Pointing to the mess on the floor, I asked, 'The noise, the broken lolly jar ... what happened?'

Now unable to deny any longer, Riley tried to *blame*: 'It was Liam.'

'Liam was in the lounge room with me when the crash happened, Riley. Answer that and stay fashionable.'

Running out of options, Riley quickly and cleverly tried *justification*: 'I was just trying to get a black jellybean for you, Dad. I know how much you like them and it all just went horribly wrong and ...'

'Nice try, Riley. You know that you have to ask us before you go to the lolly jar. So I'll ask again. What happened?'

At this point Riley realised that the only option left was to *quit*. So he ran into his bedroom and hid until he assumed it was safe to come out. He knew it was safe because the door to his bedroom opened just enough for him to survey the area and check if it had been cleaned up. Then he sent out his toy car across the floor, working on the theory that if the car made it, it should be okay to come out.

Let's summarise these responses to a bad situation:

- denying
- blaming
- justifying
- quitting.

We call these *victim behaviours*, because this is what 'victims' do. They say things like 'I am a victim of circumstance' or 'Bad things always happen to me' or 'I'm not responsible'.

Children aren't the only ones who exhibit victim behaviours. Perhaps you know some people (perhaps even you yourself) who have been known to react in such a way:

- *Denying*: 'Problem? What problem? Everything is fine!'
- *Blaming*: 'Well, if management would just wake up' or 'What they don't understand is …' or 'They are just hopeless at …'
- *Justifying*: 'I know that I should be doing it that way, but I'm going to continue doing it this way because …' or 'It's too cold to start exercising today.'

We have all worked with people who have quit, but haven't had the decency to resign. They still rock up each day, doing the bare minimum. They don't care, they don't contribute and yet they have the audacity to collect a pay cheque. How rude!

It is important to note that victim behaviours are human. We all use them from time to time when we lose our wallet, right through to when we lose a loved one. Perhaps these responses are there to protect us from being overwhelmed by the volume and scale of some of life's misfortunes.

When you lose your wallet, the first reaction is often to deny that it is lost. We look in our suit pocket or handbag again and again; we check the car for the fifth time. We don't want to accept that it is gone.

I can remember being at a friend's funeral. The widowed husband was behaving in a relatively normal manner, organising people and catering and giving a speech without choking or breaking into tears once. It would be easy to observe his behaviour and assume that either he didn't really love her, or that he was unusually strong. Neither was the case … he was denying the reality of what had happened until he had the time and space to deal with it.

Blaming, justifying and quitting can also be steps in the path to acceptance. These are human responses and we are experiencing our full humanity when we have these feelings and are able to recognise them.

By themselves, however, these reactions will not resolve the issue. They do not lead to an objective examination of the causes, ourselves or others, they do not allow us to learn and they do not help us move on.

There is an alternative to victim behaviour.

Response-ability

Writing 'responsibility' as two words gives us insight as to the word's meaning. Responsibility is about our *ability* to *respond*. This highlights two key components of responsible behaviour:

1. *Response* implies that you have a degree of control (as opposed to reaction).

2. *Ability* implies an action, skill or behaviour. This is not what you know, or what you believe, but what you *do*.

Sure, stuff happens (you may know that saying with a different 's' word). That being said, it is not what happens that really matters; it is how you are able to respond when it happens that matters.

It is at this point that I'm reminded of the wonderful truism and widely loved serenity prayer from Reinhold Niebuhr:

> *Grant me the courage to change that which I can,*
> *the serenity to live with that which I cannot, and the*
> *wisdom to know the difference.*

When we revisit the following diagram it becomes evident that some of this is 'that which I can' and some is 'that which I cannot':

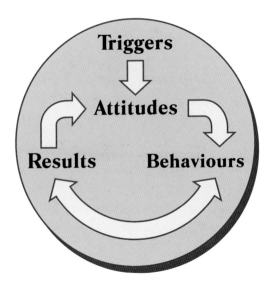

Reinhold Niebuhr may well have been saying:

> *Grant me the courage to change my* **attitudes** *and* **behaviours**, *the serenity to live with the* **triggers** *and the* **results**, *and this book to help me know the difference!*

Triggers for a good day

I promised that we would come back to these and so here we are. What are the triggers for a good day?

I have been asking groups of people to name the triggers for a bad day and the triggers for a good day for more than five years now and there is a clear pattern. People have little trouble thinking of triggers for a bad day. The examples come thick and fast and are often hilarious.

Then, when the same people are asked to identify the triggers for a good day there is often a long stretch of silence as people's brains go into a search that seems to come up with very little.

What most people do find as good-day triggers are usually external and they rely on others to do something first. For example:

- the kids get off to school with a minimum of fuss
- you get a phone call from a friend
- someone says something nice about you.

While these are all valid triggers that will lead to a more buoyant attitude, the drawback of only having external triggers is that we lose the opportunity to increase the number of good days we have. So let's list a few triggers that we can have control over:

- the kids get off to school with a minimum of fuss because you organised everything the night before
- you phone a friend
- you say something nice to a colleague or even a stranger
- you listen to your favourite music or podcast
- you create the time to exercise
- you organise a group of people to be in the same place at the same time
- you give someone you love a kiss
- you watch some comedy on YouTube.

Mapping your good and bad days

In the exercise below, take a moment to think of a specific situation that might lead to a bad day and a situation that might lead to a good day. Use these to identify your triggers, attitudes, behaviours and results.

As you do this, notice what happens in your head and in your heart when you are asked to analyse these moments in time in this way.

Triggers

In this space, identify what you might see or hear that would lead you to start thinking 'Today is going to be a bad/great day.' Be specific. Some examples are given.

How I do a bad day	How I do a great day
	For example: • you hear your favourite song on the radio • you arrive at work already knowing the first thing you will do and you get that done • you arrive at work early and have time to start things without interruption • you make someone laugh and smile.

Attitudes

In this space, identify what you are thinking and feeling when the above triggers happen. Be as specific as possible – perhaps even quote yourself.

How I do a bad day	How I do a great day
For example:	For example:

How I do a bad day

For example:

- 'Uh-oh, here we go again.'
- 'I'm always responding to stupid emails. I never seem to be able to get anything substantial done.'
- 'Here they come. I hope it's not me that stuffed up. They look like they are out for blood again.'

How I do a great day

For example:

- 'I love that. That is so cool.'
- 'Done! Great. What's next! Today's going well.'
- 'Ah! Here comes Peta, I love talking to her.'

Behaviours

In this space, identify how you behave when you are thinking the above thoughts. Be specific.

How I do a bad day	*How I do a great day*
For example:	For example:
• rolling your eyes, sighing, slumping your shoulders, shaking your head and frowning	• smiling, eye contact, eyes wide open, nodding and leaning forward
• hesitate on starting. Asking yourself questions such as 'Should I do this now or should I do that first?'	• finishing something or at least getting it as far as you can at this point before moving onto the next thing
• find reasons to not start now. Saying 'That's a really big project. I'll start that when I have more time.'	• repeating a personal mantra like, 'Just do it!', 'There's no time like the present' or 'This is not a dress rehearsal.'

Results

In this space, identify what happens when you behave that way. Consider the results from a variety of different angles.

How I do a bad day	*How I do a great day*
For example:	For example:
• quantity of output, quality of output, speed of output • costs • other people's responses • team values • the message you send to others about what you are like to work with.	• quantity of output, quality of output, speed of output • costs • other people's responses • team values • the message you send to others about what you are like to work with.

What happens now?

I am not suggesting that by writing out your triggers and attitudes, the trigger or the bad thing will stop happening. Remember that many triggers are things we cannot change and therefore need to learn to live with.

What we are doing here is looking at the following:

- how we respond when things happen
- what we can do to reduce the number and occurrence of perpetual triggers for a bad day
- what we can do to increase the number and occurrence of triggers for a great day
- how we can change our thoughts, feelings and behaviours to get better results for ourselves and for those around us.

With this in mind, in the space below, list what it was like for you to analyse these moments this way:

For me, this exercise highlights how ridiculous some of my reactions have been and how they have only served to make the situation worse. It also highlights how I may not have made the most of my time on Earth to this point. A humbling experience! Now that I know the difference, perhaps I should learn how to change my attitude and behaviours ...

That's all very well Rod, but ...

I can understand that at this stage you might be thinking a number of things to yourself. For example:

Yes Rod, but not all happiness needs to be expressed. I can be happy without having to behave like an extrovert on speed.

Or ...

Yes, Rod, fine. But perhaps life is about experiencing the highs and the lows. Perhaps life is about balance or contrast and being 'happy' all the time is not necessarily the ideal life.

Or ...

That's all very well, Rod, but aren't there just some days that are destined to fail? You know, some days when the brain doesn't seem to produce the right chemistry, the synapses don't line up, the central nervous system seems to have gone on strike? Some days the effort is all too much.

Let's address these valid concerns, one at a time.

Yes Rod, but not all happiness needs to be expressed. I can be happy without having to behave like an extrovert on speed.

I agree! Happiness that is expressed too much is called mania, and maniacs will very soon experience the opposite to happiness when people no longer want to be around them. On top of this, there are people who are exceptionally happy but do not necessarily have to express it externally.

There are a number of different paths to happiness: Taking part in easy, pleasant activities; taking part in activities that require skill and challenge; and/or taking part in activities that help others and contribute to society.

Imagine that you are watching a good movie while drinking your favourite drink. Are you running about like a rabbit on heat? No! Are you having a good time? Yes!

Imagine that you are reading your kids a good book before they go to sleep at night. Are you prancing about like a parading pony? No! Are you having a good time? Yes!

There are also activities that are associated with being fully engaged, such as playing a sport, playing a musical instrument, solving a complex problem, creating, writing and drawing. These activities require an equal match of skill and challenge, and we lose sense of time and self as we become totally focused on the activity.

During these activities you are not necessarily overtly expressing your happiness at the time and yet these activities can lead to some of the happiest moments in our lives.

There are also activities that are associated with meaning and contribution. Packing hampers for less fortunate people on Christmas Eve, helping out at the RSPCA, making sick children in hospital laugh, volunteering your time and skills. You contribute to something greater than yourself and the intrinsic reward lasts a lifetime.

So it is correct to say that not all happiness is hedonistic or extroverted. Some of the best days that we have involve passing through difficulty, focusing effort, expending great amounts of physical and emotional energy and even self-sacrifice.

Whether the activities are pleasant, engaging or meaningful, all these activities require the courage to change what you can, the serenity to live with what you cannot change and the wisdom to know the difference.

If you are watching a movie and the phone rings, you have no control over the trigger (the phone ringing) but you have complete control over how you answer the phone. When playing a sport, the final whistle is blown and your team has lost. You have no control over the final result anymore, but you do have complete control over how you respond to the other team and the loss. You may have very little control over the health of a child in the long term but you make a phenomenal difference to the child in the here-and-now when you volunteer your time to make a sick child laugh.

Yes, Rod, fine. But perhaps life is about experiencing the highs and the lows. Perhaps life is about balance or contrast and being 'happy' all the time is not necessarily the ideal life.

Once again, I agree! I'm certainly not arguing that everyone should be happy (in a hedonistic sense) all of the time. Remember that happiness also involves passing through difficulty, focusing effort, expending great amounts of physical and emotional energy and even self-sacrifice. Try asking a marathon runner at the 35km mark if he or she is happy.

It is true to say that the unexamined life is not worth living, but it is equally true to say that the unlived life is not worth examining. Some of the people who would report feeling the most happy and satisfied with their life would be people who have gone through great hardship … and endured. Think of some of the world's greatest artists, composers and philosophers. Many of these people experienced what most of us would call almost impossible circumstances. Beethoven's father was an alcoholic and a bully. The poet John Keats was orphaned at a young age and unable to marry the love of his life due to his own illness. Socrates was condemned to death for being a threat to the Athenian way of life and forced to drink hemlock! And this is to only name a few.

So yes, life is about contrasts, and perhaps the happiest people are those who have been able to best cope with these contrasts by … having the courage to change what they can, the serenity to live with what they can't and the wisdom to know the difference.

That's all very well, Rod, but aren't there just some days that are destined to fail? You know, some days when the brain doesn't seem to produce the right chemistry, the synapses don't line up, the central nervous system seems to have gone on strike? Some days the effort is all too much.

I could not agree more. Some days are certainly harder than others and some days seem to be so hard that trying isn't worth it for whatever reason.

I would ask you, however, that just before you decide to not try, to ask yourself this question: *'What are the implications of not trying for today?'* If you are happy to accept the answer to that question then I would strongly encourage you to take the phone off the hook, roll over and pull the doona over your head.

It is a wise person who will more fully experience all that life has to offer when they sit with their emotions and examine them rather than always trying to fight them.

If you choose to do this then I would congratulate you for learning acceptance!

In Chapter 2

So, to summarise Chapter 1, we could say that knowing the difference between what we can and can't change will help us in all aspects of life. We cannot change triggers and we do not have complete control over the results we generate. In most cases, what we can control are our attitudes and behaviours.

In Chapter 2, we look at what we can do to change the way we think about what has already happened. We look at how we can increase our resilience and optimism, and how to change our attitudes.

Your thoughts

Your thoughts

Two.

INTERRUPTING THE PATTERN

'Between stimulus and response there is a space. In that space is our power to choose our response. In our response lies our growth and our freedom.'

Viktor Frankl, neurologist,
psychiatrist and holocaust survivor

How to change your attitude

There is an excellent book called *Learned Optimism* by Dr Martin E.P. Seligman. This is not a new-age 'prepare for rebirthing by aligning your chakras and feng shui-ing your bathroom' type book. It is the result of many years of studies and experiments in clinical psychology. Its conclusions are highly respected in the academic and psychological community and many individuals would testify to a better, happier life today as a result of learning the skills outlined in the book.

Martin Seligman has proven that optimists live longer, experience fewer health problems and are wealthier. Whether this is a cause or effect is not known and is probably of less importance. What is important is that there is an undeniable correlation. One goes with the other.

So what is the benefit of thinking pessimistically? Well, there is one career where pessimistic thinking will serve you better than optimistic thinking and that is as a lawyer. And if you think about it, it makes sense. A lawyer's job is to think of all of the worst-case scenarios, all the things that could go wrong no matter what the probability and then prepare you, the client, for that possibility. There is also a growing body of evidence to suggest that pessimists tend to be more accurate! This explains why, when you are trapped with these people at a barbecue or dinner party, the whole experience can be a little unsettling. Next time you find yourself in heated debate with a dyed-in-the-wool pessimist you can always finish the conversation with, 'You might be right but I'm going to live long and prosper!'

As we shall see later, I'm a great believer that for the vast majority of behaviours there is a context where the behaviour is useful and a context where the behaviour isn't useful. So by using Seligman's tools I'm not advocating that everyone should always be optimistic.

Pessimism is a wonderful skill to be able to use in the following contexts:

- when planning to avoid risk
- when planning to increase your level of safety and security
- when empathising with people who are angry, upset or annoyed
- when you wish to use melancholy as a muse for creativity.

Optimism perhaps would be more useful in these contexts:

- when you are trying to achieve something
- when you want to inspire others
- when you wish to use happiness as a muse for creativity
- when you want to improve the way you feel about yourself and your situation.

So assuming that you would like to increase your health, wealth and happiness you might be interested in Martin Seligman's work.

Seligman found that helplessness is learned. If you rob people of the opportunity to help themselves often enough they will no longer try to help themselves. Even when the situation changes and helping themselves would work, people stop trying. They learn how to be helpless.

Doubtless you have seen this where you work. People who have tried a number of times to achieve something have been thwarted by powers greater than them and finally have become so cynical and pessimistic that they stop trying. Many of these people not only stop trying, they also want to stop others trying as well. Phrases such as 'That won't work', or 'We've tried that and it didn't work' and 'You can't do that' are often heard coming from the mouths of people who have learned helplessness in the workplace.

The interesting thing about cynical people is that if they just fine-tuned their behaviours a little they could radically change the perceptions of their performance and value. Notice the difference in your response to the following statements:

Trial A: 'We can't do that because ...'

Trial B: 'If we head down this path, something we'll need to consider is ...'

If I continually use comments such as the one in Trial A, I'm more likely to be labelled as a dinosaur, a road block, someone who is in desperate need of retirement.

If I use comments such as the one in Trial B, I'm more likely to be called wise, experienced and valuable.

The same piece of information could follow both half sentences in Trials A and B but which first half I choose will dramatically change the way the audience receives the information. More on changing behaviours in the next chapter … Let's get back to what Dr Seligman found about resilience and optimism.

Dr Seligman found there is a pattern that forms with people who are resilient (people who are slower to learn helplessness) and people who are not resilient (people who are quicker to learn helplessness). Some people seem to have the ability to bounce back from bad events, while others dwell on them and allow them to become an excuse for not trying.

The pattern has to do with the way people describe the event to themselves. The specific words they choose to use will either help increase their resilience or actively work against it. It is the language, not the trigger or event, that will make you resilient and optimistic. As Shakespeare wrote, 'There is nothing either good or bad, but thinking makes it so.'

The language used will have the following elements to it:

- permanence
- pervasiveness
- personalisation.

Let's look at these one at a time.

Permanence

There are two subsets to permanence:

- permanent
- temporary.

Negative Trigger – Pessimist – Permanent

When a negative trigger or event happens, the pessimist will use words such as *all*, *always*, *every*, *never* and *is*. These words are permanent words and when they are used they indicate that the person perceives the negative trigger or event to be unchangeable and constant.

For example:

- 'All managers are frustrated dictators.'
- 'Clients will always want more and management will always want to give less.'
- 'Every time I try I always stuff it up.'
- 'Diets never work.'
- 'Work is a chore.'

Negative Trigger – Optimist – Temporary

When a negative trigger or event happens, the optimist will use words such as *lately*, *this time*, *in that meeting* and *when*. These words are temporary words and when they are used they reflect that the person perceives the negative trigger or event to be fleeting, momentary and a one-off event.

For example:

- 'My manager has been acting like a frustrated dictator lately.'
- 'That client was obviously having a rough day.'
- 'I stuffed it up this time.'
- 'Diets don't work when you eat out a lot.'
- 'Work is a chore when you don't like what you are doing.'

Positive Trigger – Pessimist – Temporary

When a positive trigger or event happens, the pessimist will use words such as *once*, *just that time*, *in that meeting* and *today*. These words are temporary words and indicate that the person perceives the positive trigger or event to be fleeting, momentary and a one-off event.

For example:

- 'My manager is listening to me for once!'
- 'You can please some of the clients some of the time.'
- 'Finally! I got it right for once.'
- 'Make hay while the sun does shine.'
- 'Work went well today.'

Positive Trigger – Optimist – Permanent

When a positive trigger or event happens, the optimist will use words such as *all*, *alwcys*, *every*, *never* and *is*. These words are permanent words and indicate that the person perceives the positive trigger or event to be unchangeable and constant.

For example:

- 'My manager is always doing her best.'
- 'I'm good at dealing with difficult clients.'
- 'This is easy.'
- 'This diet is working.'
- 'That's why I love my job!'

Pervasiveness

There are two subsets to pervasiveness:

- global
- specific.

Negative Trigger – Pessimist – Global

When a negative trigger or event happens, the pessimist will use words such as *all*, *I'm* or *any*. These words are global words and reflect that the person perceives the negative trigger or event to be pervading all other aspects of their life.

For example:

- 'All politicians are corrupt.'
- 'I'm repulsive.'
- 'Books are useless.'
- 'I'm no good.'

Negative Trigger – Optimist – Specific

When a negative trigger or event happens, the optimist will be more specific. Specific words and sentences reflect that the person perceives the negative trigger or event to be compartmentalised into a one-off event or associated with one person/thing.

For example:

- 'Fred Nerk is corrupt.'
- 'She finds me repulsive.'
- 'This book is not what I'm looking for.'
- 'I seem to be struggling today.'

Positive Trigger – Pessimist – Specific

When a positive trigger or event happens, the pessimist will be more specific. Specific words and sentences reflect that the person perceives the positive event to be compartmentalised into a one-off trigger or event, or associated with one person/thing.

For example:

- 'I'm pretty clever with that stuff.'
- 'My kids did well in their last maths exam.'
- 'I think she likes me.'
- 'I was making him laugh.'

Positive Trigger – Optimist – Global

When a positive trigger or event happens, the optimist will use global words and sentences. Global words reflect that the person perceives the positive trigger or event to be pervading other aspects of their life.

For example:

- 'I'm pretty clever.'
- 'My kids are good at maths.'
- 'I'm an attractive person.'
- 'I make people laugh.'

Personalisation

There are two subsets to personalisation:

- internal
- external.

Negative Trigger – Pessimist – Internal

When a negative trigger or event happens, the pessimist will use words such as *I*, *I'm*, *me* or *my*. These words are internal words and reflect that the person perceives the negative trigger or event to be linked to themselves.

For example:

- 'I caused that.'
- 'I'm not creative.'
- 'I'm poor.'
- 'If it wasn't for me …'
- 'My impatience got in the way.'

Negative Trigger – Optimist – External

When a negative trigger or event happens, the optimist will use words such as *you*, *they* or *it*. These words are external words and reflect that the person perceives the negative trigger or event to be linked to an external person, place or thing.

For example:

- 'You're stupid.'
- 'They are hopeless.'
- 'I'm not very lucky at cards.'
- 'I grew up in a poor house.'

Positive Trigger – Pessimist – External

When a positive trigger or event happens, the pessimist will use words such as *you*, *they* or *it*. These words are external words and reflect that the person perceives the positive trigger or event to be linked to an external person, place or thing.

For example:

- 'You're the reason we won.'
- 'I was lucky.'
- 'We had Jessica on our team and she's fantastic.'
- 'They were laughing.'
- 'I was brought up in a wealthy house.'

Positive Trigger – Optimist – Internal

When a positive trigger or event happens, the optimist will use words such as *I*, *I'm*, *me* or *my*. These words are internal words and reflect that the person perceives the positive trigger or event to be linked to themselves.

For example:

- 'I'm a lucky guy.'
- 'What helped was my ability to …'
- '… my wealth …'
- 'I make people laugh.'

Please note: There is a clear difference between depression and personal responsibility. People who are depressed will need to externalise the causes of negative events to assist with their recovery. People who are not depressed need to take responsibility for their actions. Sometimes optimists do cause bad things to happen and sometimes good things happen without optimists. We are concerned in this book with the pattern of language you use to describe things to yourself and how this influences your behaviours.

I'm sure that you can see how someone continually using the same pattern of pessimistic language to describe what happens to themselves or to others could very easily become cynical, and lead them to give up trying and become depressed.

Revisiting your maps of a bad and good day

With what we have learned about the language of optimism and resilience, let's revisit the section where you identified triggers, thoughts and feelings and what your attitude would be when bad-day and good-day triggers happen.

As you revisit the words you chose to describe the triggers and your attitude to those triggers, notice your internal talk. Identify words that indicate permanence (permanent/temporary), pervasiveness (global/specific) and personalisation (internal/external). Please do not be concerned if you cannot find as many as I have outlined below in the example. If you have only used a sentence to explain your attitude, try expanding that to a paragraph and see where that leads.

Triggers

How I do a bad day

For example:
- I (internal) have hundreds of emails (global).
- Murray (external) walks towards me (internal).
- Jean's number comes up on my phone. Jean (external) is calling me (internal).
- My (internal) 'to-do' list is ridiculously long and weeks old (global).

How I do a great day

For example:
- I (internal) hear my (internal) favourite song (specific) on the radio.
- I (internal) arrive at work knowing exactly (specific) the first thing I (internal) will do and I (internal) get that (specific) done.
- I (internal) make someone (external) laugh and smile.
- Someone (external) at work pays me (internal) a compliment.

Attitudes

How I do a bad day

For example:
- I (internal) hate my job. Every morning is the same (global permanent). Hundreds (global) of stupid emails that I (internal) have to (permanent) answer. Will this ever end? (global permanent).
- Damn! Here comes Murray again (permanent). I know what it will be about. It's always (permanent global) about what I (internal) haven't done (global). He'll start to lecture me like it was my fault (permanent global).

How I do a great day

For example:
- I (internal) love that. That is so cool. I (internal) always (permanent) feel good when I (internal) listen to that (external temporary) song. I (internal) reckon I (internal) could play the guitar riff (specific) on that song with a little practice.
- Done! Great. What's next! Today is (temporary) going well (global). I (internal) love it when I (internal) get things done (global). That (specific) was not as hard as I (internal) thought it was going to be.

Attitudes

How I do a bad day

He (external) drives me crazy (internal) with his continuous (permanent) whinging. Nothing is ever (global permanent) going to be good enough for that guy (external).

- No! Not Jean! I'm (internal) too busy (global). Every time (global permanent) she (external) phones me (internal) it's always (permanent) about something that is so trivial and stupid (global). She (external) is a vacuum that is constantly (permanent) sucking up my (internal) attention. I (internal) can't afford to waste any time (global) with her (external). I (internal) have bigger fish to fry (global).

- I hate work (global). I (internal) never (permanent) seem to make any (global) headway with my (internal) 'to-do' list (specific). The stuff (global) on it is weeks even months old (global). All (global) I (internal) ever (permanent) seem to be doing is fighting other people's (external) fires (global). I (internal) never (permanent) get time to do what I (internal) want (global), what I (internal) need (global).

How I do a great day

In fact that (specific external) was pretty easy. How often does that happen? You (external) worry about something (global) before you (external) start and then you (external) actually start it and it turns out to be much simpler than you (external) thought. That happens a lot (global).

- That (external) was funny. Where did that (external) come from? Some days (temporary) the brain (external) just seems to be functioning better (global) than others I (internal) guess. Today (specific temporary) is one of those days. Let's make the most of it (external temporary). I'll (internal) see who else (global) I (internal) can make laugh today (temporary).

- That's (external) nice. It's nice that she (external) noticed what I (internal) did (specific) and my contribution (global). I (internal) worked hard on that (specific) and I (internal) felt good about what I (internal) did (specific) so it's nice that others (external global) noticed it (specific) as well.

How to increase your resilience

Now that we have identified the components of our self-talk (our attitude) in terms of permanence, pervasiveness and personalisation, we are ready to look at how we can toy with these attitudes to increase our resilience, to increase the usefulness of our behaviours and ultimately improve our results.

Seligman identifies some excellent tools to help reduce pessimism and increase optimism and resilience. These are:

- dialogue
- disputation
- distancing
- distraction.

Dialogue

When you are thinking in a way that is not going to help you feel resilient, write down the words you are using and identify the elements of permanence, pervasiveness and personalisation. Try to reword the dialogue using the opposite subsets of each category, then notice the difference.

Using one of the examples above:

> *I hate work (global). I (internal) never (permanent) seem to make any (global) headway with my (internal) 'to-do' list (specific). The stuff (global) on it is weeks even months old (global). All (global) I (internal) ever (permanent) seem to be doing is fighting other people's (external) fires (global). I (internal) never (permanent) get time to do what I (internal) want (global), what I (internal) need (global).*

In this example where the trigger is negative, the following words were used:

- Permanent words = 3
- Temporary words = 0
- Global words = 8
- Specific words = 1
- Internal words = 6
- External words = 1

We could reword this using the opposite subsets and it might sound like this:

> *Three things (specific external) have happened today (temporary) that made it difficult to make some headway with my 'to-do' list. Twenty per cent (specific) of the items on my 'to-do' list are more than four weeks old. I (internal) will schedule in three hours this afternoon (specific temporary) and find a place where they (external) won't be able to find me (internal). No interruptions (external) will mean I (internal) can get the first three things (specific) on my 'to-do' list done.*

The trigger is still negative but the words used are as follows:

- Permanent words = 0
- Temporary words = 2
- Global words = 0
- Specific words = 4
- Internal words = 3
- External words = 3

Or …

> I (internal) helped Graham (external) fix 'X' (specific),
> Patricia (external) with 'Y' (specific) and helped Chris
> (external) avoid 'Z' (specific). And it is only 10am
> (specific).

It is easy to imagine how the second and third statements are far more likely to help us deal with the same situation in a more resilient way.

Disputation

The best form of defence is attack! When you hear yourself thinking in a way that is not going to help you feel resilient, question the accuracy of every word. Imagine that you are your own devil's advocate and argue against the thinking: All? Every? Can I think of a time when that wasn't the case? Can I think of what I did/didn't do that helped? What evidence do I have to the contrary? How many alternatives can I create? Is this useful?

One of the above examples is:

> I (internal) hate my job. Every morning is the same
> (global permanent). Hundreds (global) of stupid
> emails that I (internal) have to (permanent) answer.
> Will this ever end? (global permanent).

There are dozens of ways to dispute the accuracy of this statement. For example:

- 'I hate my job …' – The implication here is that you have *always* hated your job. So we could test that by asking:
  - Can you think of a time when you liked or even loved your job?

- Is it possible to conceive that there could be a time in the future when you might like or even love your job again?
- *'I hate my job …'* – The implication here is also that you hate every aspect of your job. So we could test that by asking:
  - Can you identify aspects of your job that you do like?
  - What does your job allow you to do that you like?
  - What have you achieved in your job that gives you a sense of satisfaction?
  - What aspects of your job help other people or contribute in a meaningful way?
- *'Every morning is the same …'*
  - Every morning? When did you last arrive at work and not dwell on the number of emails you got?
  - The same? What was different about yesterday?
- *'Hundreds of stupid emails …'*
  - How many exactly?
  - Which emails are not stupid?
  - Which emails are important?
  - Which are interesting?
  - Which are entertaining?
- *'… that I have to answer …'*
  - How many do you delete without having to take action?
  - How many do you delete without even having to read?
  - How many do you pass on to others without answering?
  - Who else can answer them?
  - What would happen if you didn't answer that one? What about that one? And that one?

- *'Will this ever end?'*
  - Will what specifically ever end?
  - Who is responsible for ending it?
  - What are your alternatives?
  - What would happen if it did end?
  - Is that what you really want?

So in that statement of 22 words we have been able to dispute it on at least 23 different levels. How accurate is this statement really? Face it, you are talking crap.

Distancing

When you are 107 years old and on your death bed you are probably not going to be thinking to yourself, 'If only I said ...', and if you are you will need help ... but by then it will be too late.

The skill here is to put some perspective on what is going on. How important is it really?

Here is a list of questions and statements that will help to put things in perspective:

- When you are 107 years old will it matter then?
- If the world was going to end tomorrow would you care about what just happened?
- Is it a fact or just a belief?
- Who is worse off than you?
- What are all the things that could happen that would be worse than this event?
- Where would be a worse place to be at this moment?

- What would happen if you did/didn't? How much does that really matter?
- What do you have in your life that this will not affect? What is really important in your life? For example:
  - family?
  - friends?
  - house?
  - purpose?
  - hope?
  - dignity?
  - self-esteem?
  - your life?
  - your health?
  - your sense of self?
  - your belief?
  - your faith?

Distraction

When you are thinking in a way that is not going to help you feel resilient, interrupt the pattern by saying or doing something totally unpredictable.

Try feeling angry, upset or down while you are tilting your head to one side, poking your tongue out as far as you possibly can, crossing your eyes, waving your arms and hands about frantically and hopping as high as you can on one leg. If you succeed at doing this and staying angry, upset or down, you might need professional psychological assistance … seriously!

So next time your boss walks towards you and you find yourself launching into a pattern that you do not want to continue, you now know what to do.

In Chapter 3

To summarise Chapter 1 of this book we could say that knowing the difference between what we can and can't change will help us in all aspects of life. We can't change triggers and we don't have direct control over the results we generate. What we can control, in most instances, are our attitudes and behaviours.

In Chapter 2 we looked at what we can do to change the way we think about what has happened. We looked at how to increase our resilience, how to become more optimistic and how to change our attitudes.

In Chapter 3 we will look at how to increase our behavioural flexibility, how to increase the number of times our responses to situations and people are ideal, how to reduce the number of times we think to ourselves, 'If only I'd said ...' or 'If only I'd done that ...', and how to reduce the stress and frustration associated with 'I could never do that' and still maintain a strong sense of self.

Your thoughts

Your thoughts

Your thoughts

Three.

BE WHAT YOU WANT TO SEE

'You must be the change you want to see in the world.'

Mahatma Gandhi, political and spiritual leader

I arrived home one evening and I was hungry. So I looked in the fridge to see what I could find. The fridge was close to empty with just a half-dead, overripe tomato sagging in the ironically named crisper. I closed the fridge and looked in the pantry. But there was nothing in there that was going to be fast enough, tasty enough or good enough. So what did I do? I went back to the fridge! Maybe something had cooked itself in the meantime …

There is a popular definition of insanity that goes, 'Insanity is doing the same thing over and over and expecting a different result.' By this definition, we have all been insane.

Using the new platform that changing our attitude has given us, we can now look at how to do the following:

- increase our behavioural flexibility
- increase the number of times our responses to situations and people are ideal
- reduce the number of times we think to ourselves 'if only I'd said …' or 'if only I'd done that …'
- reduce the stress and frustration associated with 'I could never do that'
- maintain a sense of self.

List three words

Imagine that it is your funeral. You have died and somehow you have been allowed to come back just for the eulogies. You are able to hear the people who knew you the best describe you and your life. What adjectives would you most like them to use?

If that image is a little too raw for you, try this one. Imagine that it is the day after you have left your current workplace. You have moved on to bigger and better things but, before you left, you installed a webcam in the tea and coffee area where your workmates gather. They are talking about you now that you are gone and remembering what it was like to work with you. Once again, what adjectives would you most like them to use when describing you?

Here are a few examples that you might like to choose from:

- decisive
- driven
- creative
- extroverted
- calm
- friendly
- empathetic
- supportive
- firm but fair
- optimistic
- strong sense of justice
- persistent
- accurate

- fun/funny
- enthusiastic
- family oriented
- helpful
- engaging
- successful
- happy
- relaxed
- motivated
- strategic
- centred
- always present
- deep
- smart
- quick

So, what are your three words?

1.

2.

3.

The power of association and mental rehearsal

Let's just put those words to the side for one moment. We will revisit them later.

A friend of mine used to teach children at a local high school. She sometimes looked after the detention group, the group of kids that had been in trouble at school during the week and had to stay behind after school as punishment.

One kid seemed to always be on detention. He was a little creepy and often in trouble. This friend of mine often found herself alone in the detention class with this kid, so to pass the time she would ask him questions to try and find out how his brain worked.

One day she asked him, 'So what type of films do you watch?'

He replied, 'I like horror films.'

'Like what?' she dug.

He proceeded to list some very scary films: 'Friday the 13th, Nightmare on Elm Street, Child's Play.'

'How do you watch those films? When I watch them I get scared.'

'Well you're an idiot then.'

'What do you mean?'

'Well, who are you being in the film?'

When most of us watch a horror film we associate with the victim. In our mind we are saying things like, 'No! Don't go in there. Just leave and call the police.' It turns out that what this kid was doing was associating with the perpetrator of the horrific acts. Inside his head he was thinking to himself things like, 'Okay. Don't start the chainsaw up yet. They are nearly in the house. Wait ... wait ... NOW!'

Frightening, isn't it!

The point being, when we read a book or when we see a film, we associate with one of the characters. A great way to highlight this is to watch a film that has multiple storylines. Films such as *Pulp Fiction*, *Crash* or *Love Actually*. As you watch these you will notice an increased level of association and interest when a certain storyline comes back on screen. We often think something like, 'Ah! Good. This person again. I was wondering what was happening with them.'

This association is a very powerful thing. Monkey see monkey do – we learn from watching others. We needed to be able to do this on an evolutionary level because if we were to survive as a cooperative species we needed to be able to read other's responses and know what these meant for us. If someone looking over your shoulder shows shock and runs away, the message is clear.

Recent research into neuropsychology shows us how this works in the brain. When we observe someone doing something our brain fires the same neurons that would be required to carry out the task ourselves. So, for example, when we watch someone grab hold of a cup our brain fires the same neurons we would have to fire if it were us grabbing hold of the cup.

This principle has been used in sports psychology for many years. An integral part of becoming an elite athlete is to mentally rehearse.

There are a couple of famous studies to highlight this. In one study, gymnasts who were to learn a new move were divided into two groups. One group was instructed to visualise themselves being able to do a particular move, while the other group was given no instructions. A couple of weeks later, when the time came for them to do this particular move, without the benefit of any previous physical practice the group who visualised had a 50–60 per cent success rate, whereas the group that had not visualised had, initially, only about a 10 per cent success rate.

In another study, a basketball team was split into two groups in order to practise free throws. One group physically practised making the shots. The other group was instructed to mentally practise by visualising that they were making the shots. Then the two groups competed with each other to see the improvement. Now I would love to be able to tell you that the group who visualised was the better group. It wasn't. What is astonishing, however, is that the players in this group improved almost as much as the players who had practised. Leading sportspeople, of course, will both mentally rehearse and practise. Michael Jackson talked about how a large part of his learning to dance was watching endless footage of Fred Astaire.

The challenge for us mere mortals is to notice what we are mentally rehearsing. When we are asked to perform something that we perceive to be outside our competence, we often imagine the worst and then mentally rehearse that. If we asked someone to speak at a conference, many people would imagine themselves in front of the audience like a rabbit in headlights, forgetting content, stuttering, shaking like a washing machine on spin cycle and with a highly visible heat rash exploding from neck to face. Then they would run this film over and over in their head, mentally rehearsing ways to fire all the neurons that make this wonderful experience come true. This is how to 'do' worry. Think of a situation in the future, imagine it being the worst possible outcome just so we can feel sick about it now. Ridiculous but very human.

Elite athletes do not line up at the beginning of the 100m sprint thinking to themselves, 'I'm no good at this. I don't even know why I bother. I'll come last. I'll probably pull a hamstring, fall over and embarrass myself.' Elite athletes have been schooled in the art of imagining the best possible outcome for them and mentally rehearsing that. They are thinking: 'I'm going to get my start right, I'm going to keep my head up and I will beat my best time.'

Imagine how well your day would go if you could apply these principles we have just discussed!

In order to do this we need to find a role model, someone who does those three words you wrote down at the beginning of this chapter really well. We need to observe them doing those words and we need to ask ourselves some questions as we are watching them. We can then identify how to behave in order to increase the likelihood that others will describe us in the same way.

Micro-behaviours

Let's work on one example. Say, for the sake of argument, that you would like others to describe you as *decisive*. The fact is that you cannot 'do' decisive. What you can do, however, is a series of micro-behaviours that, when someone observes you doing them, would lead them to describe you as decisive. It is these micro-behaviours that we are looking to list.

To do this we need to ask ourselves a couple of questions:

1. What would you see someone do or hear someone say that would lead you to describe them that way?
2. How exactly do you do that? What would you see someone do or hear someone say that would lead you to describe them that way?

Yes, I know I have repeated the question. I have done so for a reason. When we try to answer the first question it is easy to come up with labels and not micro-behaviours. For example, if I asked the question, 'What would you see someone do or hear someone say that would lead you to describe them as decisive?', chances are I would get responses such as, 'They would be quick thinkers, they would know the answer.' These are useless to us because we cannot copy them. So we need to ask ourselves again,

'How exactly do you do that? What would you *see someone do* or *hear someone say* that would lead you to describe them that way?'

The answers to these questions will need to fall into one of the following categories to qualify as micro-behaviours:

- *Language*: Choice of specific words over other possible words.
- *Tone of voice*: The combination and movement of volume, pitch and speed in what you say.
- *Gestures*: How you move your hands, body and face.

Using these three pointers and drilling down with the question, 'What would you *see someone do* or *hear someone say* that would lead you to describe them that way?', we will find the micro-behaviours of 'decisiveness'. For example:

- Language:
  - use definitive words such as must, have to, can't, should, three, seven
  - avoid possiblity words such as might, could, possibly, perhaps, couple, several.
- Tone of voice (the combination and movement of volume, pitch and speed in what you say):
  - talk slowly to avoid the use of 'um' and 'ah' and other gap-fillers
  - use a downward inflexion at the end of your sentence.
- Gestures:
  - count points off on your fingers as you explain each one
  - turn your palms down as you gesture
  - avoid gesturing too much, avoid visual noise
  - Use a non-specific pointing gesture.

Individually these micro-behaviours are trivial and meaningless. Used together they form a pattern and that pattern would lead me to describe you as decisive.

There are a couple of tools that will help us develop other examples. These are:

- Satir Categories
- Vocal variety.

Satir Categories

Virginia Satir, the great American family therapist, identified five different body-language patterns used under stress.

What she noticed from years of observation is that there are some classic body gestures that are often combined with a certain language, and that these send a very clear message to other people about what is being said.

These gestures can be used as a basis for building our micro-behaviours, communicating with greater congruence and increasing the likelihood that people will describe us a certain way.

As we describe each gesture, imagine that you are on the receiving end of someone using each gesture and notice what you would be thinking or feeling. Keep in mind that this might reveal which gestures you already use as a preference and therefore which gestures you might add in order to increase your behavioural flexibility.

An important note is that every gesture has a place and a time. There is no one gesture that is inherently good or bad. All gestures can be used appropriately and inappropriately; the skill is to know when and how much to use each one.

The Blamer

Often gesticulating with one hand or a pointing finger, the Blamer can be used to make a strong point. Overused (especially when combined with a blaming tone), the Blamer posture can provoke other people, or make them feel as if they are wrong. The Blamer is very useful in increasing assertiveness. Notice that the effect of the Blamer can vary considerably depending on the accompanying facial expression. We often associate the Blamer with a frown and a shaking of the head. Notice how different it would be if the Blamer had his or her head on a slight angle with a cheeky grin and wide eyes.

The Placater

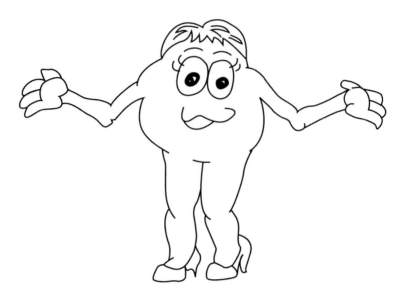

This gesture is usually arms outstretched with the palms facing up. The Placator allows the communication to be more humble, open and non-threatening. It is useful in highly emotional situations or to demonstrate an obvious fact. The Placator can also be used to avoid conflict. Warning: If the Placator is overused, the other person may feel as if you are being weak or overly apologetic.

The Super Reasonable

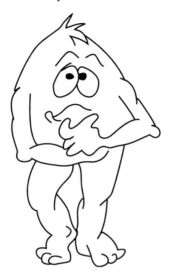

Using a thinking posture, with one hand under the chin and the other folded across the chest, the Super Reasonable category is useful for communicating logic or facts, or when wanting to prompt thought in you or your audience. It can also be used to suggest that you are listening and taking in what the other person is saying. It is also handy for giving the impression of being very reasonable! Warning: If the Super Reasonable is overused the presenter can come across as cold and unemotional. There is less warmth in this stance.

The Distracter

Notice how the name is similar to one of Seligman's tools for interrupting a pattern. The Distracter is not typified by any particular posture, rather by many different postures at nearly the same time! Often categorised as a dizzy or confusing character, the Distracter is very useful for humour. Many of the best comedians in the world use a physical or verbal version of the Distracter to get people to laugh. The Distracter is great for breaking or changing your state or the state of the audience. It is also useful when you want to liven up an audience. Warning: If the Distractor is overused the presenter can seem unpredictable and difficult to follow and the audience will get tired.

The Leveller

The Leveller is characterised by a palms-down gesture and an even stance. It can be done by moving the palms from the centre of your body to the sides of your body in a 'this is final' gesture. This often gives the impression of fairness or cutting to the chase. The Leveller is terrific for making a strong point without blaming. Another version of the Leveller is to gently drop the palms down in a calming gesture. This is useful for dissolving any issues and settling people down. Overdone, the Leveller can lead the audience to think the presenter is only interested in the bottom line and is reluctant to let people vent.

So, to continue with our example (of being seen to be decisive), we could say that the Blamer and the Leveller would be the most useful. Certainly the Distracter and the Placator will not help us come across as decisive.

This is a tool that helps with what we do. Now we need to look at a tool that will help with the way we speak.

Vocal variety

Vocal variety asks you to consider the tone of your voice. Tone is often seen as a difficult thing to quantify and yet there are quantifiable aspects to tone. These are as follows.

Speed

Some people prefer to talk fast. Some people like talking slowly, and there are all the shades of grey in between. You can imagine what it is like when a fast talker meets a slow talker.

Slow talker: 'So ... I found myself ... feeling ... that ... well ... I was ...'

Fast talker (impatiently finishing the slow talker's sentence for them): 'Frustrated? Annoyed? Upset?'

Slow talker (sick to death of fast talkers finishing their sentences for them): 'No. Not so much frustrated ... more ... irritated.' (which is essentially the same as frustrated but *I* will finish *my* sentence, thank you!)

Volume

Some people have a voice that can carry through walls and doors. They don't consciously talk loudly, it's just how they talk. Others talk softly. A *Seinfeld* episode illustrated this well. It featured Kramer's girlfriend who was a 'low talker'. Jerry was sick of asking her to speak up so he just said 'Yes' to something she asked him and, the next thing he knew, he had agreed to wear a puffy pirate shirt on television.

Pitch

For some people, the voice comes from high in the throat. This is often associated with excitement and enthusiasm. There are others whose voice seems to come from their ankles. The voice of James Earl Jones as Darth Vader's in *Star Wars* comes to mind. Some people have a high-pitched voice; some have a low-pitched voice and again there are all the shades of grey in between.

Vocal variety is about noticing the combinations and movements of these quantifiable aspects of tone to generate a certain response in other people.

So let's continue our example of being seen to be more decisive. As Australians, many of us have the tendency to have an upward movement or inflexion at the end of our sentences. You use an upward inflexion when you want to ask a question. So we associate an upward inflexion with uncertainty. Therefore a downward inflexion would send a message of certainty and decisiveness.

To complete our example, we can see that if we combine the words we use (must, have to, can't, three, seven) with the gestures we use (Leveller, Blamer) and the tone of voice we use (downward inflexion at the end of the sentence), we can create a powerfully decisive message.

Try saying the following using the micro-behaviours identified above to see how decisive you come across: 'There are three things we must consider before we are able to make the final decision. These are language, tone of voice and gesture.'

Micro-behaviour dictionary

Jim Loehr is a world-class performance psychologist who has worked with professional tennis players to try to identify what makes the difference between top-ranked and lower-ranked players. After watching hours and hours of video he noticed a couple of interesting things. Firstly, there is little difference between stroke, strength and court coverage. The difference that Jim discovered was that the top-ranked players spent time in between points recovering from the previous point and preparing for the next point, while lower-ranked players would move straight to the next point without recovery time.

Jim would have been using the same observation skills that we have looked at to identify this point of difference. This is powerful stuff and is used by the world's best coaches. They observe top performers closely and then fine-tune performance at the micro-behaviour level.

My aim is to build a micro-behaviour dictionary, where people can type in an adjective and out pops a list of skills they can replicate.

Think of all the times in life when this would be useful. You have a hot date that you desperately want to impress. You have spent time and money on your hair, clothes and face and now you can visit a website that will provide you with a list of suggested words, tone of voice and gestures to use to generate the best impression.

You have an interview for your dream job. You have updated your résumé, dry-cleaned your interview suit and now you can visit a website that will provide you with a list of suggested words, tone of voice and gestures to use to create the right impression.

It is the third time today an idiot has cost you time and money. Instead of decking the guy, now you can visit a website that will provide you with a list of suggested words, tone of voice and gestures to use to best get your message across.

This website is currently being built and will, over time, develop into an amazingly easy-to-use, yet practical website. Below is an extract from the *Micro-behaviour Dictionary* that I have built. The full version is available at this website:

www.microbehaviourdictionary.com

The aim is for you to think of a word that you would like to be, or to be described as being, and the *Micro-behaviour Dictionary* will list the language, tone of voice and gestures that align with that description.

Please feel free to use it as you see fit. All I ask is that if you copy it or re-use it in any way, you include the following: 'Reprinted with the kind permission of Rod Matthews & Impact Human Performance Technologies.'

I have also included a group of micro-behaviours called 'other'. These are ways of thinking that will make the behaviours come more naturally.

Calm / Centred / Relaxed / Deep

Language:

- Speak less
- Allow others to talk first
- Avoid emotionally packed words like *wow*, *fantastic*, *amazing*, *horrific*, *dreadful*, etc
- Use phrases that understate rather than overstate, for example 'We seem to be having a little difficulty at the moment' rather than 'Oh @#*>@$, we are stuffed!'
- Use measured words such as 'Let's consider …', 'We might do well to think about …', 'First let's regain our composure …'

Gestures:

- Use Leveller gestures
- Use fewer gestures
- Maintain a small, relaxed smile on your face
- Do not react to external stimulus immediately

Tone of voice:

- When you do speak, do so with a slower speed, a lower pitch and a softer volume

Other:

- Consider the stimulus and the possible responses to the stimulus before responding
- Notice what you are feeling and label that feeling in your mind (not out loud)

Creative / Inspirational / Imaginative

Language:

- Use phrases such as 'What about ...', 'What would happen if ...', 'Imagine if ...', 'Hypothetically speaking...', 'Shooting from the hip ...'
- Use possibility words such as *might*, *could*, *possibly*, *perhaps*, *couple*, *several*
- Avoid definitive words such as *must*, *have to*, *can't*, *three*, *seven*
- Accept other people's ideas and add to them by using phrases such as 'What I love about what you said was ...', 'Imagine if ...', 'What I think is great about that is ...', 'What would it be like if we added ...'

Gestures:

- Show enthusiasm for others' ideas by having your eyes wide open, leaning forward, and nodding as others are talking
- Show enthusiasm for your ideas by using a visual aid (whiteboard, flip chart) to explain you idea
- Use Distracter gestures

Tone of voice:

- Use a faster, slightly louder and slightly higher pitched tone of voice

Other:

- Prepare to be creative. Before the meeting or time when you would like to be creative, think about the current problem and reword the problem into a statement of what you need. For example, a statement of a problem might be: 'We have a problem with decreasing profit.' Turn this into a statement that identifies what you want: 'To increase profit.' Then imagine that there are over 50 ways to increase profit and build a list of as many ways as you can think of. For more information on how to do this, go to the members' section at www.impacthpt.com.au and download the article entitled *Try Thinking Creatively for a Change*

Friendly / Engaging / Sociable

Language:

- Ask people questions about themselves
- Encourage them to keep talking by saying things like *Mmm*, *Uhuh*, *Ohh*, *Alright*, etc
- Ask people questions that are linked to what they just said.
- Use polite words such as *please*, *thank you* and *excuse me*

Gestures:

- Show that you are interested by maintaining eye contact about 60–70 per cent of the time
- Reflect the appropriate emotion clearly on your face. If the person is talking about something that is exciting, show excitement. If the person is talking about something that is sad, show sadness
- When you hear something that you have in common, show enthusiasm for what they are saying by widening your eyes, showing a surprised expression on your face and saying something like, 'Me too!'
- Use Distracter and Placator gestures
- Avoid Blamer and Leveller gestures

Tone of voice:

- Use a slightly higher pitch and a faster speed

Other:

- Listen for areas that you have in common
- Ignore or avoid areas of significant difference between you and them
- Do not talk until it is your turn to talk. Watch for a signal from the other person that indicates they have finished, then talk about what you have in common on the topic, what you can agree with, what you can understand. Avoid talking about what you disagree with, or what you thought was wrong

Empathetic / Supportive / Compassionate

Language:

- Use feeling words that reflect the other person's emotions, for example *annoying, fantastic, horrible, great, frustrating, disappointed,* etc
- Avoid words that judge the other person, for example *no, yes but, you're wrong, you're being silly,* etc
- Use phrases that validate what they are feeling, for example 'No wonder you felt ...', 'That is perfectly understandable', 'If that happened to me I would be ...'

Gestures:

- Reflect the appropriate emotion clearly on your face. If the person is talking about something that is exciting, show excitement. If the person is talking about something that is sad, show sadness
- Use Placator gestures
- Avoid Blamer gestures

Tone of voice:

- Talk more slowly with a lower pitch and a softer volume
- Increase the variety of pitch in your voice

Other:

- Look and listen for cues of emotion in what the other person is saying
- Think about when you have felt that way and label the feeling, then reflect that label to the other person using a sentence such as 'That would be so annoying' or 'That must have been fantastic.'
- Do not talk until it is your turn to talk. Watch for the signal that indicates they have finished, then talk about what you have in common on the topic, what you can agree with, what you can understand. Avoid talking about what you disagree with, or what you thought was wrong

Persistent

Language:

- Use words such as *finish*, *complete*, *finalise*, *conclude*, *end*, *focus*, *concentrate*, *apply*. Avoid Distracter phrases such as 'What about …', 'What would happen if …', 'Imagine if …', 'Hypothetically speaking …', 'Shooting from the hip …'
- Use definitive words such as *must*, *have to*, *can't*, *three*, *seven*
- Avoid options-based words such as *might*, *could*, *couple* or *several*
- Use the assertiveness technique known as 'broken record'. When people ask you what you are doing, have a one-sentence response that you repeat

Gestures:

- Use the posture that you use when you are working
- Keep your eyes focused on the task and reduce eye contact with other people
- Frown in a way that looks as though you are concentrating
- Use Blamer, Leveller and Super Reasonable gestures
- Avoid Distracter and Placator gestures

Tone of voice:

- Use a slower, softer and lower tone of voice

Other:

- Identify what triggers distraction, then remove or reduce these triggers. When the triggers still happen, notice that it would normally distract you and then get back to what you want to persist with
- Identify the triggers that lead to the skill you would like to persist with. When those triggers happen, remind yourself that this is an opportunity to practise persistence and get on with it

Accurate

Language:

- Use exact words such as *precise*, *specific*, *exact*, *particular*, *defined*, *detailed* or *definite*
- Avoid ambiguous words such as *generally*, *largely*, *many*, *most*, *often*
- Use phrases such as 'It's not that simple', 'The complexity here is …', 'What we need to know is …'

Gestures:

- Use an emotionless expression – a poker face
- Avoid Distracter and Placator gestures
- Use Blamer gestures to point at things, not people

Tone of voice:

- Use less variety in your pitch
- Speak slightly slower

Other:

- In your mind, take the topic you wish to be accurate on and divide it into as many subgroups and sub-subgroups as you can. For example, food has these subgroups: meat, vegetables, fruit, legumes, dairy, processed, organic. Just looking at the subgroup of meat, we could build the sub-subgroups of 'domestic meats' and 'wild meats'. Then, taking the sub-subgroup of domestic meats, we could build another subgroup including beef, chicken, lamb and pork. *Then* we could take the subgroup of beef and divide it into Angus, Shorthorn, Kobe, Hereford – I think you probably get the idea by now

Fun / Funny / Witty

Language:

- Use understatement or overstatement
- Increase your use of description, adjectives and adverbs – words and phrases such as *wiggled, popped, elephant-sized, ridiculous-looking*
- Increase your use of words that describe things in different senses, such as 'It sounded like …', 'It looked like …', 'It smelt like …', 'It felt like …' (Don't step in it!)

Gestures:

- Exaggerate your gestures and facial expressions
- Use Distracter gestures

Tone of voice:

- Talk a little faster and a little louder
- Use a wide variety of pitch
- Emphasise the unusual words
- Toy with a single sentence and find all the different tones, inflexion and emphasis that you could use to say the words in that sentence

Other:

- Use similes and metaphors to explain things
- Toy with the context of what you are saying. For example, the statement 'The boy threw the stone' could be true in many different contexts: In a schoolyard, at a window, across a lake, at a snake, at his mate Jake, at a drake. Each time we change the context it provides a totally different meaning and generates a different response in the audience. Toy with this until you find a humorous one

Strategic / Visionary / Leader

Language:

- Use global words and phrases such as *most*, *all*, *every*, *never*, *'the pattern here is …'*
- Use a future-based language: 'In the future we will…', 'In two to five years …', 'Where we need to be …', 'outlook', 'potential', and 'opportunity'
- Avoid a past-based language: 'In the past', 'In my experience', 'The way we have…'
- Use definitive words: *must*, *have to*, *can't*, *three*, *seven*
- Avoid possibility words: *might*, *could*, *possibly*, *perhaps*, *couple*, *several*

Gestures:

- Use Placator and Leveller gestures
- Avoid Distracter gestures
- Use fewer gestures

Tone of voice:

- Talk more slowly to avoid the use of 'um' and 'ah' and other gap-fillers
- Use a downward inflexion at the end of your sentences
- Use a moderate variety of pitch
- Use a slightly louder volume

Other:

- Read articles in the press that talk about the future and the direction of the economy, politics, the arts, society, your industry, etc. Talk about what you have read
- Look for patterns and cycles in statistics. Talk about what you have noticed
- Extend the direction of the patterns you have noticed to suggest what the future holds

Helpful / Cooperative

Language:

- Use words and phrases such as 'Yes', 'I can ...', 'I will ...', 'What I can do is ...', 'What can I do to help?', 'What else needs to be done?', 'How are you going today?', 'How are you going with...?', 'How about if I ...?', 'Would you like me to ...?', 'No problems', 'Easily done'
- Avoid words and phrases such as 'No', 'I'm unable to ...', 'Sorry'

Gestures:

- Use Placator gestures
- Avoid Blamer gestures
- Smile as you talk
- Lean forward
- Look people in the eye

Tone of voice:

- Increase the variety of pitch
- Talk a little louder and slower

This is by no means intended to be a definitive list and I'm not suggesting that just because you do the listed micro-behaviours once that you will suddenly become a totally different person. Like learning anything worthwhile, two things are true for these micro-behaviours: there is no *one* thing, and you'll need practice and persistence.

There is no **one** *thing*

Around the time of the Beijing Olympics I was listening to the radio and Scott Volkers, head of Queensland Swimming at the time and the coach of a number of Olympic champions, was being interviewed. He was being asked the questions that you often hear being asked during the Olympics: 'How fast can we actually swim?', 'What is the limit of the human body?', 'How can we continue to break records?' He gave an excellent answer and pointed out that there is no one thing that allows us to continue to break records. There are lots and lots of little things. For example: The chemical composition of the water that was present in the pool at Beijing is superior to the chemical composition of the water in the pool at the LA Olympics. When I first heard this I was reminded of the swimmers being interviewed when the new pool for the Sydney Olympics was opened. The swimmers were all saying that it was a 'fast pool'. I thought at the time: 'How can a pool be fast? It doesn't move, it weighs tonnes and it is concreted into the ground.' Apparently this is the sort of thing they were referring to.

What we now know about lane ropes and their ability to smooth the water and reduce wake is superior to what we knew during the Munich Olympics. Our ability to record and correct stroke from under the water as well as from on top assists as well. Even, and I know this is a little controversial, the swimsuits and the buoyancy they add helps.

So there is no one thing that allows us to break records. There are lots of tiny things that on their own are almost meaningless. And yet, if we can string enough of these together we will have a point of difference. It is the same with micro-behaviours. Not one of these micro-behaviours will result in you being labelled anything specifically. But if you can string enough of these micro-behaviours together you will have a point of difference.

Practice and persistence

Imagine that we were coaching a boy to play tennis. If at the first training session we lined him up to play against Roger Federer, chances are he would leave thinking that tennis is a stupid game and most certainly not the game for him. This is because the level of challenge has far exceeded the level of skill.

Recognising our mistake, we ask the child to come back and we reduce the level of challenge by just taking a bucket of tennis balls and one by one asking him to see if he can watch the ball onto the racquet and connect.

After doing this for one or two training sessions the child is now starting to enjoy tennis and feels more confident about his skill level. So we decide to stick with the bucket of balls trick. After the third or fourth training session something will happen. The boy will now start to become bored with tennis. His level of skills now exceeds that challenge provided by the bucket and balls and, unless we can increase the challenge level, he will probably beg his parents to find him another sport.

Unless you are lucky enough to have a great coach, you will need to notice your own responses and manage them in order to ensure that it is easy and rewarding to practise and persist. Are you anxious about practising? In that case perhaps you need to reduce the challenge level a little. Are you bored? In that case, up the ante on yourself.

Your three words

This brings us to the three words you identified at the beginning of this chapter: words you would like others to use when describing you. Your task now is to use the tools above to build a list of micro-behaviours that you could use to lead others to describe you that way.

- **Word 1:** _____

  Language:

  Tone of voice:

  Gestures:

  Other:

- **Word 2:**

Language:

Tone of voice:

Gestures:

Other:

- **Word 3:**

Language:

Tone of voice:

Gestures:

Other:

In Chapter 4

To return to the original quote …

Grant me the courage to change what I can, the serenity to live with what I can't and the wisdom to know the difference.

In Chapter 1 we identified that we can change our attitudes and behaviours but we cannot change the triggers or the results.

In Chapter 2 we found that Dr Martin Seligman's tools of dialogue, disputation, distancing and distraction enable us to change our attitude.

Now in Chapter 3 we learned a technique to help us change our behaviours, to increase the likelihood that people will see us in the way we would like to be seen.

In Chapter 4 we will talk about how to develop the 'serenity to live with what we can't change' – the triggers and their results.

Your thoughts

Your thoughts

Four.

SERENITY AND ACCEPTANCE

How to go with the flow

'Muddy water, left to stand, will clear.'

Anonymous

Why are serenity and acceptance so difficult?

We can answer this question by looking at it from two angles:

- our individual mind – the brain/central nervous system
- our collective mind – society.

Our individual mind – the brain/central nervous system

In order to understand why practising serenity and acceptance is not easy, we need a quick lesson in the anatomy of the brain. The *Triune Brain* is a model proposed by Paul D. MacLean, where components and functions of the brain are grouped into three key areas:

The Neocortex

The Limbic System

The Reptilian Brain

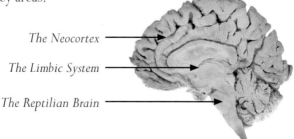

The Reptilian Brain is largely responsible for the survival functions, control of our muscles, our balance and our automatic functions such as breathing and heartbeat. Without the Reptilian Brain you would need to have your iPod permanently plugged into your ears repeating the phrase, 'Breathe in, breathe out.'

The Limbic System primarily looks after the slightly more advanced functions of long-term memory, smell, attachment and emotions. It includes the amygdala, which performs a primary role in the processing and memory of emotional reactions, and fight, flight and freeze responses.

The Neocortex is involved in the higher functions of vision and the processing of sound. It generates motor commands and does most of our spatial reasoning, conscious thought and language processing.

Fortunately, you have a model of the brain on the end of your arm. A good way to remember most of this is to make a fist with your hand. Your arm is the brain stem that carries all the information to and from the brain, your thumb is the Reptilian Brain, your palm is the Limbic System and your fingers form the Neocortex.

So that is the anatomy lesson, but how does this work in relation to triggers, attitudes, behaviours and results?

When your boss walks towards you with that look, when your partner raises his or her voice, when the kids are testing the outer limits of your patience, when there is a trigger that we would class as negative, the Reptilian Brain and amygdala take over, flooding the body with chemicals that prepare us for fight, flight or to freeze.

This is fantastic if we are in a life-threatening situation. When our ancestors were on the plains of Africa competing with lions, leopards and hyenas, having a part of our brain that made decisions in an instant that then floods the body with the appropriate chemistry to respond accordingly was just what we needed. If we had an overdeveloped Neocortex and an underdeveloped Limbic System it could be argued that we would not have survived. Thinking to yourself, 'Hmm, a lioness seems to be stalking me but before I can make a decision as to how to respond I should conduct an experiment to see if my hypothesis is correct' will not keep you alive.

While this is true in life-threatening situations, many of us are lucky enough to live in stable and developed nations, with laws, a police force and relatively few dangers. Your boss walking towards you with that look, your partner raising his or her voice or the kids testing the outer limits of your patience might be stressful but you are probably not going to end up injured or dead as a result. In these situations it is our chemistry that often leads us to overreaction and wishing later that we'd said or done something different. Often we wished we had stayed calm.

So, one reason why serenity and acceptance are difficult is that we are automatically using our survival chemistry for non-life-threatening situations.

Another reason why it is difficult to achieve serenity and acceptance is that our central nervous system is surrounded by many other central nervous systems ... our society.

Our collective mind – society

In Western/Anglo-based societies such as the United States, Britain, Canada, Australia and South Africa, we mostly find ourselves in a 'meritocracy'. A meritocracy is a society that rewards those who have demonstrated talent and competence through past actions or by competition. We reward these talented and competent people with wealth, position and social status. In my opinion, there are, of course, notable exceptions to this rule: the Hilton sisters, the Kardashian sisters and 99 per cent of the cast of Big Brother. My opinions and these exceptions aside, our society sends us a message about merit, telling us that if we have influence (wealth, position and social status), we are of higher value.

One of the principles behind the types of activities that are rewarded is that being in control is preferable to relinquishing control, and taking action is preferable to acceptance. This is not true in all the world's cultures but in Western/Anglo cultures it is pervasive.

For instance, for issues such as security, the environment, politics, famine, acquisition, ownership, justice and education, society suggests that choosing to accept (rather than to change) the current situation means there is something wrong with you. You should want to take control and take action and we are bombarded with this message on a daily basis through advertisements, movies, books, magazines, news reports, television shows, myths and legends, political decisions and promotions in organisations. Much of the subtext to these reinforces a preference for taking control.

This relentless messaging creates the context in which we live. We pick up these messages (consciously and unconsciously) and they influence our behaviours and our values, no matter how 'strong minded' we like to think we are.

There is an excellent book called *The Tipping Point* by Malcolm Gladwell. In it, he explains the power of context. He suggests that we are not consciously aware of the context in which we find ourselves, and yet this has a dramatic effect on our behaviours. To illustrate this, he talks about the 'Broken Windows' theory which:

> … *was the brainchild of criminologists James Q. Wilson and George Kelling. Wilson and Kelling argue that crime is an inevitable result of disorder. If a window is broken and left unrepaired people walking by will conclude that no one cares and no one is in charge. Soon, more windows will be broken and a sense of anarchy will spread from the building to the street on which it faces, sending a signal that anything goes.*

Gladwell then goes on to recount how in the mid-1980s, Kelling was hired by the New York Transit Authority to make the subway a safe place for commuters and to increase the number of people who used the service. Kelling enacted his Broken Windows theory by introducing a zero tolerance for broken windows, slashed seats and graffiti on train carriages. If a train carriage was damaged in some way the policy was to have it repaired straightaway and to have only the best carriages in operation. The clean-up took from 1984 to 1990, after which crime on the New York subway declined dramatically.

So, the context in which we find ourselves sends a message that influences our behaviours. If we are surrounded by the message that society will reward us if we successfully take control and achieve, this makes it even more difficult to practise acceptance. Acceptance and serenity, in this respect, are the opposite of control and achievement.

It is little wonder that some people find it difficult to practise serenity and acceptance.

What can we do?

So far in this book we have examined the question, 'How do you do a good day?' In the process, we have identified that perhaps a good day is when we change what we can, live with what we cannot and have the wisdom to tell the difference.

We recognise that it is possible to change our attitudes and behaviours, but not the triggers or the results. We have also found some practical tools to help change our attitudes and behaviours.

What is left is to identify how to develop the serenity to accept what we can't change: to accept the triggers and their results.

We have already covered a number of tips, tools and techniques to help increase your serenity. Let's review them.

What we can and cannot change: just knowing the difference

You may have been to a lecture or presentation and walked out at the end thinking to yourself, *'What a waste of my time. I already knew all that ...'*

In this example, the presenter only talked about the known.

You may have been to a lecture or presentation and walked out at the end thinking to yourself, *'Were they speaking English? I didn't understand any of that ...'*

In this example, the presenter only talked about the unknown.

A good lecture or presentation is when the presenter is able to link the known to the unknown. This is how we make meaning. We can understand something when we are able to link it to something we already know.

When this happens, we experience a 'Eureka!' moment. It is easier to feel comfortable with something we know and understand than something that is totally foreign to us.

With this in mind, just knowing the difference between what we can and cannot change will help increase our levels of comfort and serenity.

What we **can** *change*

In Chapter 2 of this book, we discussed the tools that Dr Martin Seligman has identified as being able to assist us with changing our attitudes. These tools will also help us increase our level of serenity as they enable us to shape our own thoughts and responses to things that happen.

The four tools that Seligman identifies to help us increase our serenity are:

- *dialogue*: The ability to recognise our own self-talk and reword it

- *disputation*: The ability to question and test the accuracy of negative self-talk
- *distancing*: The ability to put what is happening into perspective. Some of the most relaxed, satisfied and centred people I know have developed this ability
- *distraction*: The ability to significantly shift our mood by distracting ourselves in the moment. This reduces the amount of time and energy we spend on negative responses.

What we can change: using the behaviours of serenity

In Chapter 3, we looked at the idea that we can control our behaviours. So let's look at how to behave in a serene manner:

- Language:
  - speak less
  - allow others to talk first
  - avoid emotionally packed words such as *wow*, *fantastic*, *amazing*, *horrific* or *dreadful*
  - use phrases that understate rather than overstate: 'We seem to be having a little difficulty at the moment' rather than 'Oh @#*>@$, we're stuffed!'
  - use measured phrases such as 'Let's consider …', 'We might do well to think about …' or 'First let's regain our composure …'
- Tone of voice:
  - when you do speak, do so more slowly, at a lower pitch and softer volume.

- Gestures:
  - use Leveller gestures
  - use fewer gestures
  - maintain a small, relaxed smile on your face.
- Other:
  - do not react immediately. Consider the stimulus and the possible responses to the stimulus before responding
  - notice what you are feeling and label that feeling in your mind (not out loud).

These are the behaviours of acceptance and serenity, and they will help you come across to others as accepting and serene. Sometimes this is not enough, however. Sometimes we would like to actually be serene and feel acceptance as well. How do you 'do' that? Well, perhaps the question is best answered by first looking at why acceptance is difficult.

Who are the experts at serenity and acceptance?

So, if serenity and acceptance are difficult because of our individual and collective mind, what hope have we got? Is it ever possible to be serene and accepting? The answer is, of course, most definitely, yes! There are serenity and acceptance experts out there, people who could represent their country at the next 'Serenity and Acceptance Olympics'. These are Buddhist monks with over 2500 years of investigating the workings of the mind and how to live with that which we cannot control. Western scientists are beginning to take an interest in the practices of Buddhist monks and, in particular, the practice of meditation.

Dr Richard Davidson at the University of Wisconsin, Dr Paul Ekman of the University of California and Dr Dan Siegel of Harvard University are just a few of the growing number of neuroscientists, neurologists, psychologists and psychiatrists who have amassed an impressive amount of research in this field.

Chances are that we can all build an image of a Buddhist monk being very centred, serene and accepting, and able to keep his cool while all others around him are losing control. Experiments have been carried out that show some meditation practitioners can achieve a state of inner peace even when facing extremely disturbing circumstances. For example, Dr Paul Ekman tells the story of jarring noises (one as loud as a gunshot) that failed to startle the meditating Buddhist monk he was testing. Dr Ekman said he had never seen anyone stay so calm in the presence of such a disturbance.

Other studies use imaging devices to show what happens in the brain during meditation. Using these, we have been able to study the effects of Buddhist practices for cultivating compassion, equanimity and mindfulness.

For centuries Buddhists have believed that pursuing such practices seems to make people calmer, happier and more loving. At the same time they are less prone to destructive emotions. It turns out that we can now explain what practising Buddhists have known for centuries, using Western scientific language.

The science of meditation

To understand the benefits of what is happening in the brain while meditating or practising mindfulness, we need to add a little more to our earlier lesson on anatomy. So bear with me as I explain this, and I will translate it into English afterwards!

There is a smaller part of the Neocortex called the Medial Prefrontal Cortex. This is located just behind your forehead. For the sake of space and ease we will call it the mPFC. According to Dr Siegel, this part of the brain is essential for serenity and acceptance. Research on mice and humans reveals that the mPFC produces a chemical called GABBA-A that floods the amygdala and counters the chemicals produced in the fight, flight or freeze response.

In plain English, what this means is that we can effectively deal with the brain chemistry that puts us into fight, flight or freeze mode using our own brain chemistry, which comes from another part of the brain, the mPFC. This brain chemistry extinguishes the fight, flight or freeze response and allows us to respond in a more measured and considered way.

Using imaging devices, we are able to see that when people meditate regularly they are exercising the mPFC and have a greater ability to produce the chemical that allows them to extinguish the fight, flight or freeze response.

How to meditate

Some meditation principles

When first starting to meditate you might find that your mind doesn't want to cooperate. It wants to show you re-runs of a recent embarrassing or annoying moment. It wants to list the stuff you should be doing, complete with deadlines, and then nag you for not moving. It wants to ask you important questions like whether the bathroom would look better in Baker's White or Forest Green. You then tell yourself, 'Stop it! I'm trying to meditate!' So your mind quietens down for all of 10 seconds before wandering again.

After this happens for a while it is easy to start to think something like, 'I'm no good at this. It's not working.' This thought increases your levels of frustration. Next thing you know you've decided that this meditation thing is all too difficult, and it seems to be the opposite to relaxing, so you decide to go for a trip to the hardware store.

A couple of principles might help here.

1. Stable not empty

Meditation is about making your mind stable and calm, not about trying to empty your mind. It is about the *focus* of your intention and attention, not the *content* of your intention and attention.

So when pictures and thoughts enter your mind, notice what you are doing first and then label this softly and slowly in your mind. Say things like 'thinking, thinking', 'remembering, remembering', 'judging, judging.' By the time you have finished the label, the thought will have been stabilised and calmed, and may even have gone.

2. It's not what you expect, it's what it is

I'm not sure exactly what I expected when I first started meditating. Perhaps some sort of mystical experience where senses were at once non-existent and omnipresent as I was astral travelling with the infinite … or something like that.

There are expectations on a macro and micro level that reduce the quality of the meditation experience. Macro-expectations are expectations about meditation itself, its benefits, its ease and its after-effects. Micro-expectations involve thinking things such as *I should*, *they should*, *I'm not*, *they're not*, *I am* or *they are*. During meditation, these micro-expectations manifest themselves in the form of '*I shouldn't* be distracted', '*I shouldn't* have any pain there' or '*I'm not* relaxed.'

Separating the expectation (what you expect) from what you are experiencing (what it is) will allow the meditation to be what it is without your judgement. Label what *is* gently in your mind without the expectation. For example: 'thinking, thinking', 'discomfort, discomfort' or 'relaxed, relaxed.'

Practising this in meditation increases our ability to do the same outside meditation. This is a key serenity and acceptance technique that we will revisit in more detail later.

Now that we have these principles ready to go, let's look at a meditation process.

A meditation process

Find a quiet room where you will not be disturbed. You can sit cross-legged if you want, or sit in a chair – do whatever is comfortable for you. I recommend that you avoid lying down as meditation is not sleeping. If you feel you are becoming sleepy during the meditation, open your eyes just a little to let in some light and take a slightly deeper breath.

There are many paths to meditation. I'm currently working on the following five. I will present them in the order that I practise them. Some days I only do Levels 1 and 2 in the 10 to 15 minutes I have allocated. Other days I'm able to visit all five. Remember … it is what it is. Don't rush it. Meditation is about the practice, not the achievement.

1. Focusing on the breath

This is often the introductory level meditation. As the name suggests, this is about focusing on your breathing either by putting your attention on the sensation of air as it passes through your nostrils, or by focusing on the filling and emptying of your lungs or the movement of your belly.

2. The body scan

This involves moving your attention around your body. Pause on parts of your body that you choose and just hold your attention there. You might find pain or tension; hold your attention over that area. Label what you feel in that area, then let it release. This is fantastic for relaxation and healing.

3. Awareness of awareness

This is where you focus your attention and intention on the process that regulates the flow of energy and information. In other words, you become aware of what you are aware of. The sound of a car passing, the sound of people outside, the memory in your head, the thought, the judgement … notice what you are noticing, and perhaps label what you are noticing.

4. The spaces between

After practising awareness of awareness for a while, you might start to find that there are gaps in between the thoughts, memories and images. The aim now is to try and focus your intention and attention on these gaps.

5. Your choice

Before you start your meditation, choose something that you would like to meditate on, for example serenity, acceptance, compassion, forgiveness, love, happiness, achievement, completion or appreciation. Give these things icons, images, feelings, sounds, sentences, words or thoughts – whatever you like – and focus your intention and attention on these.

There is a large volume of research out there to suggest an inverse correlation between the size of a person's vocabulary and their propensity for violence. The suggestion is that the more difficulty a person has in expressing themselves, the more likely they are to become violent.

Meditation asks us to practise sitting with our feelings and observing them or labelling them. This increases our ability to recognise and express the feelings that we have. So if people with a low ability to recognise and label their feelings are more likely to react violently, then it only stands to reason that a person who is emotionally literate will be more able to calmly observe and respond rather than react.

If meditation is not your bag, there are some other, slightly more active alternatives:

- yoga
- tai chi
- qi gong
- even walking, swimming or running.

Either way, in a world that encourages people to focus their attention in their head or externally, some sort of meditative, mindful, introspective practice is strongly recommended. The only caveat to that statement would be that if you are suffering from depression, introspection without professional assistance is not recommended.

A final word

We have certainly covered a lot of distance together.

We know now that the phrase 'a good day' is best used as a verb rather than a noun. It is something that you 'do', not something that you own. We have the wisdom to know the difference between what we can change and what we cannot. We have some tools to help us master our own attitudes and our own behaviours. We also have techniques to help us increase the amount of serenity and acceptance in our lives.

That leaves us with one last important point to make – the information in this book is not enough. In fact, I would go so far as to suggest that knowledge is cheap and easy. The law of the markets states that any commodity of high volume tends to have a low value. You can hop on the internet and download pretty well any kind of information that you care to imagine (and many things you might care not to imagine as well). And yet with all this knowledge there is still only a small percentage of people who lead happy, significant, memorable and successful lives. Why is this the case? Because knowledge is not enough. Allow me to illustrate ...

Let us say that we went out to dinner together. Let us also imagine that the service we received from the waiter was dreadful. He was rude; we had to attract his attention to get him to come over; he mixed up our orders and didn't apologise; and he always sighed and groaned when we asked for something.

If at the end of our meal we asked that waiter, 'Do you know what it takes to provide excellent customer service?', chances are that he would say, 'Yes.' We could even ask him to sit a written customer service exam and he would probably pass with flying colours! So knowing something is not enough.

I would even go so far as to say that knowledge is useless. Knowledge is of little use until it is put into practice, until something is done with it, until it becomes a skill, until it is used. How is it that Olympic swimmers are able to swim at the level they do? Not because they have read about how to swim on the internet and sat a written exam. At some stage they got wet! How do you build skill? You practise and you persist.

But even both knowledge and skill are still not enough. Let us go back to our restaurant where we received the poor customer service. Imagine that we complained to the manager of the restaurant. The manager then went up to the waiter and said, 'Look, I've had some feedback from some customers and … well … I need you to smile.' Now the waiter knows they should smile and smiling is a skill … a micro-skill but still a skill. Chances are that the next poor customer would be on the receiving end of the biggest *forced* smile you can imagine.

We can tell when a smile is forced and that is because there is a third component to this equation and that is your *intention* as you use the skill. Are you smiling just because you have to? If so, that will come across. Or are you smiling because you honestly believe that by smiling a warm genuine smile, you will decrease the amount of complaints, increase the amount of compliments and make the whole evening more enjoyable for all concerned … that will come through in your smile too.

In order to increase the number of 'good days' that you experience in your life you will need to do more than just read this book and know how to do what's in it. You will need to *practise* the skills and you will need to practise every day with the *intention* of creating as many good days in your short life as you possibly can.

May your life be what you most desire because you had the courage, the serenity and the wisdom to make it so.

Your thoughts

Your thoughts

READING LIST

Listed below are the texts that I have drawn from in writing this book. We all stand on the shoulders of others, and I heartily recommend that you read the following books:

Learned Optimism

Martin E.P. Seligman, Ph.D.

2002 Random House. ISBN 0 09 182568 7

Yes. Optimism is a skill and it can be learned. In this book there is a questionnaire to test your level of optimism and the results will probably shock you, even if you like to think you are already a pretty optimistic person. There are also some clear principles that optimists use for you to learn.

Status Anxiety

Alain De Botton

2004 Penguin. ISBN 0 241 14238 5

Alain De Botton is a modern-day philosopher who has the amazing knack of making his philosophy understandable and applicable. In *Status Anxiety*, he talks about how we are almost hard-wired as a species to want more, to want to climb the social ladder and to want to keep up. An excellent book if you are interested in why acceptance can be difficult in our society.

The Consolations of Philosophy

Alain De Botton

2001 Penguin. ISBN 0 14 027661 0

This book makes philosophy accessible. Alain De Botton examines the work of some of the world's greatest philosophers by starting with very human issues: being unpopular, not having enough money, frustration, inadequacy, a broken heart and all the various difficulties we face. It is a great read.

Influencing with Integrity: Management Skills for Communication & Negotiation

Genie Z. Laborde

1987 Syntony Publishing. ISBN 0 933347 10 3

An incredibly detailed, insightful and skilful book. This is where I sourced the material on Virginia Satir and the Satir Categories. In the book Genie Laborde also outlines one of the best skills to dispute what you are telling yourself and that is the skill of Fluff Busting. Her expertise is astonishing!

Flow: The Psychology of Optimal Human Experience

Mihaly Csikszentmihalyi

1991 Harper Perennial. ISBN 0 06 092043 2

This book is awesome. It looks at how people can get themselves into 'the zone', the flow state. It is the culmination of years of research by Mihaly Csikszentmihalyi. It is not easy going but it is very rewarding reading.

Edward de Bono's Textbook of Wisdom

Edward de Bono

1996 Viking. ISBN 0 670 87011 0

An arrogant title … and it delivers! Edward de Bono, the lateral thinking expert, documents how differently wise people think to most people. A fascinating read.

Right & Wrong: How to Decide for Yourself

Hugh Mackay

2004 Hodder. ISBN 0 7336 1549 X

This book does not preach morals; instead it provides some tools to analyse some of the big questions around relationships, how we should live and (of course) business ethics.

An easy-to-read, practical philosophy book.

If you liked this book, find more of the same at

www.rodmatthews.com

REFERENCES

Frankl, Viktor Emil
"In between stimulus and response …"
Retrieved December 3, 2010, from BrainyQuote.com
Website: http://www.brainyquote.com/quotes/quotes/v/
viktorefr160380.html
This quote is attributed to both Stephen Covey and Viktor Frankl,
although Viktor Frankl seems the more likely source.

Gladwell, Malcolm
The Tipping Point: How Little Things Can Make
a Big Difference
Published by Little, Brown and Company, USA, 2000
ISBN-10: 0-316-31696-2
Gladwell refers to the work of George L. Kelling and Catherine
M. Coles, *Fixing Broken Windows* (New York: Touchstone, 1996)

Loehr, Jim & Swartz, Tony
The Power of Full Engagement
Published by Free Press, New York, 2004
ISBN-10: 0743226755
ISBN-13: 978-0743226752

Satir, Virginia
Peoplemaking
Published by Souvenir Press Ltd, London, 1990
ISBN-10: 0285648721
ISBN-13: 978-0285648722
Satir notes the following: 'In 1937, the Christian student newsletter *The Intercollegian and Far Horizons* attributed the serenity prayer to Niebuhr in this form: "Father, give us courage to change what must be altered, serenity to accept what cannot be helped, and the insight to know the one from the other."' [Niebuhr, Reinhold]

Seligman, Martin E. P.
Learned Optimism
Published by Knopf, New York, 1991 (Paperback reprint edition, Random House, South Australia, 2002)
ISBN-10: 0-09-182568-7

Siegel, Dr Daniel J.
The Mindful Brain: Reflection and Attunement in the Cultivation of Well-Being
Published by W. W. Norton & Company, New York, 2007
ISBN-10: 039370470X
ISBN-13: 978-0393704709

Your thoughts

Your thoughts

Your thoughts

Your thoughts

Your thoughts

Your thoughts

Your thoughts

Your thoughts

Your thoughts

Your thoughts